Happy Birthday
Grand daughter
Love
Po-Po - & Gung-gung.

Ginger Rogers did everything
Fred Astaire did, but she did it
backwards and in high heels.

Bob Thaves

girl POWER

*inspiring stories of smart,
strong, super-real women*

Published by Hallmark Books,
a division of Hallmark Cards, Inc.,
Kansas City, MO 64141
Visit us on the Web at www.Hallmark.com.

Editorial Director: Todd Hafer
Art Director: Kevin Swanson
Writer: Steve Riach
Designer: Mary Eakin
Production Artist: Dan Horton

ISBN: 978-1-59530-028-7
BOK4350
Printed and bound in China

Hallmark
GIFT BOOKS

ACKNOWLEDGMENTS

This book is the result of years of work and months of research and documentation, and I received much help from many caring people. I would like to thank the following:

My wonderful family, who gave me their constant love and support and often unselfishly sacrificed in order to allow me the necessary quiet time to write.

My terrific assistant, Kristen Martin, who spent hours researching, transcribing, and proficiently handling various tasks associated with helping to pull this book together.

The Board of Directors of the Heart of a Champion Foundation, for their commitment to seeing the stories of great people utilized to help shape character in young people all across America.

And Todd Hafer at Hallmark, who came up with the concept for this book, believed in it, and was responsible for it becoming a reality.

I also want to thank the women who are profiled here. Over the years, I have had the true privilege of interviewing and telling the stories of hundreds of people for a variety of projects. These courageous, determined, hardworking, gifted individuals, whose stories inspire millions, live so that their own experiences may inspire others. I am grateful they have chosen to trust me with their stories; it has been my sincere honor to tell them in various forms of media throughout the years.

Steve Riach

I dedicate this book to my incredible wife
and daughters, each of whom is a true and beautiful
expression of "girl power." Having overcome much
in their lives already, they are shining lights to others—
every day. Their commitment to live by conviction,
to exhibit grace, and love unconditionally is inspiring.
They have taught me so much, and I am so thankful
to share my life with them.

table of contents

introduction

Every woman has a story to tell. The women in this book certainly do. Whether they're overcoming great obstacles, persevering through tough times, or following dreams no one else thinks they can catch, their stories are sure to uplift and inspire us all. From the small-town physician who longed to give back to her community to the track-and-field star who returned to competition after a crippling disease left her unable to walk, these amazing people all have one thing in common—they're girls. And they dared to dream.

BETHANY
Hamilton

Bethany Hamilton started surfing before she could walk. As a teen sensation, she seemed assured of a long and successful future as a professional surfer. But how she would approach her future changed dramatically on the morning of October 31, 2003, when she was attacked by a shark in the waters off Kauai, Hawaii.

Bethany began that day as she did most others, surfing with her best friend, Alana Blanchard, along with Alana's father, Holt, and brother, Byron. Six other surfers were in the water with them at a spot on Kauai's North Shore known to locals as "Tunnels."

At about 7:30 a.m., a tiger shark estimated to be about fourteen feet long swam under Bethany and bit off her left arm just below the shoulder.

"Nobody saw the shark," said Bethany's older brother, Noah. One surfer had told news reporters that he heard Bethany scream and then yell "Shark! Shark!" At first, the people nearby thought she was kidding. Then they saw her trying to paddle to shore with one arm, Noah said.

Fellow surfers quickly put her on another board and began paddling her several hundred yards to shore. Holt Blanchard used a surf leash to apply a makeshift tourniquet to stop the bleeding. Doctors later said Blanchard's quick action saved Bethany's life.

Bethany was carried ashore on the surfboard and placed in a pickup truck to await an ambulance. She remained conscious. The tourniquet, direct pressure on the wound, and the effects of shock reduced the bleeding. An ambulance crew started intravenous fluids as soon as they arrived, then rushed Bethany to a nearby hospital.

"I think the biggest news is that she never cried once," said Noah. "Losing her arm will change a lot for her, but she never cried once. The doctor was amazed."

Throughout the ordeal, Bethany never lost her composure.

"My arm was hanging in the water, and it just came and bit me," she said. "It kind of pulled me back and forth. But I just held on to my board and then it let go. I looked down at the red water. Right away, I knew it was a shark and I knew my arm was gone. . . . I wasn't scared. I didn't think I was going to die or anything."

Her surfboard held the evidence: the left side had a sixteen-inch bite taken out of it.

The weekend prior to the attack, Bethany competed in a National Scholastic Surfing Association contest in Hawaii. She had been runner-up in the national championships at San Clemente, California, earlier in the summer. The homeschooled student had consistently beaten older girls and women in amateur competitions in the past two years. At just thirteen years old, the former Hawaii State champion was ranked eighth in the world and was on her way to a brilliant pro career. She already had gained a number of sponsors, including industry heavyweight Rip Curl.

"We were just trying to recruit her for the world team," said Rainos Hayes, a former pro surfer who now serves as head coach of Hawaii's world team contingent. "She's probably, right now, the strongest thirteen-year-old water woman in Hawaii: her strength in big waves, her paddling ability, her water knowledge—she's the best. Her character is such that she will overcome this."

Others wondered just how Bethany would be able to bounce back. Experts said overcoming the emotional and psychological pain of an amputation, particularly one caused by such a traumatic event, would be extremely difficult—and even more so for a teenage girl.

But, in spite of it all, Bethany was back in the water in no time. And on January 10, 2004, just ten weeks after the attack, she returned to competition.

Stunning onlookers, Bethany placed fifth in her age group in the Open Women Division of the National Scholastic Surfing Association. While she occasionally struggled to push off her board with one hand, Bethany was undeterred.

"It was definitely a good start," she said. "Once I get up on the board, I'm OK. Sometimes it's hard to get there."

She rejected special treatment. "I offered to give her more time (between heats) or put her in a more favorable heat," tournament director Bobbi Lee said. "She refused. She said she wanted to be treated like anybody else."

Despite all she's been through, Bethany has a remarkably positive outlook.

"I look at everything that's happened as part of a plan for my life," she said. "There's no time machine. I can't change it. There's a plan for my life and I'm going to go with it."

Her friend Ballard remains amazed at Bethany's emotional balance. "She stands out not just because of her surfing," she said, "but because of the kind of person she is."

LAURA

Wilkinson

Laura Wilkinson has always liked a good comeback story. "Triumphs over tragedies—I love stories like that," she said after her performance at the 2000 Summer Olympic games in Sydney, Australia.

With a gold medal draped around her neck as she stood atop the medal stand for the women's 10-meter platform diving competition, Wilkinson became one of the greatest comeback stories in Olympic history.

She was more than forty points behind after the preliminaries, but in the final competition, Wilkinson surged from fifth to first place on her third of five dives— a reverse two-and-a-half somersault, which drew four 9.5s from the judges. Then, on her fourth dive, she locked up the gold by nailing her most difficult dive, an inward two-and-a-half somersault in the pike position, which had given her lots of trouble in the prelims. Her scores were all 8.5s and 9s. She held off China's Li Na, a fierce competitor, to capture an event that had not been won by the U.S. in 36 years.

But it was how she did it that makes Laura Wilkinson's story so amazing.

That March, just five months before the games, Wilkinson broke the middle three bones in her right foot in a freak training accident: she banged it on a piece of plywood used for indoor training while practicing somersaults for the inward two-and-a-half. Wilkinson decided to delay surgery. She knew the foot would have to be re-broken and set after the Olympics, but she pressed on. A fused mass of bone at the bottom of her foot made it feel like she was walking on a rock. But her positive attitude was reflected even in her choice of clothing. She has a T-shirt with the message, "Pain is weakness leaving the body."

Wilkinson approached her precarious route to the Olympics with caution, rarely able to practice her actual dives from the platform. She did what she could on crutches for two months. She practiced six hours a day with various types of casts, mounting the platform and visualizing going through her takeoffs and come-outs for every dive on her list. When the casts came off, she wore a protective boot to cushion the climb. She performed most of her dives from a sitting position. The first time she attempted to climb the thirty-three-foot tower after the injury, it took her ten minutes to get to the top. Still, Wilkinson was determined not to let the situation sidetrack her dream. Said Wilkinson's coach, Ken Armstrong, "I had never seen that sense of urgency in her."

While her climbs to the platform did not last quite as long in Sydney, she still made them with a protective boot on her foot. When Wilkinson reached the top of the platform for her fourth dive, knowing she was one performance away from gold, she slowly removed her boot and tossed it down to the pool deck below. As her name was called, she looked out at those in the stands cheering for her and acknowledged them with a smile. She took a deep breath, then launched into the same dive that had caused her injury.

"It's the same action that I broke my foot on," she recalled immediately after her performance. "It makes me nervous as I get close to the platform. Plus, I have to stand on the ball of my foot. But I guess when it got right down to it, it didn't matter anymore. I figured I had nothing to lose."

When it was over, Wilkinson had indeed lost nothing and gained much—a gold medal and claim as world's best diver, but she gained wisdom along the way. "I knew that I just wanted to dive because I loved it," she said. "I didn't want to live my life thinking, 'What if?' I guess if you find out that if you want something bad enough . . . fear and pain become unimportant. I wanted to win a gold medal, but I knew that if I didn't, it wasn't the end of the world."

In 2008, eight years after the Sydney Olympics, Wilkinson made a comeback of a different sort. She decided to postpone retirement for one last chance to compete for her country. While she did not medal at the Beijing games, Wilkinson's presence was strong. She was named captain of the U.S. team and was frequently seen mentoring the next generation of American divers. But no one expected any less from one of the most respected divers in U.S. history.

VONETTA
Flowers

During the 2002 Winter Olympic Games, a dramatic story in the women's bobsled event seemed like the script from a soap opera, complete with elements of controversy, betrayal, and melodrama. In a historical finish, though, integrity triumphed in the end.

Team USA-1 was led by driver Jean Racine, who, along with longtime push-mate Jen Davidson, had won the previous two seasons' World Cup overall titles. The team was favored for the gold medal and, in the months leading up to the games, appeared on television commercials. There was even talk of book deals and future endorsements for the duo after they brought home the gold. But just two months prior to the games, Racine decided to part with Davidson and replace her with former collegiate track star Gea Johnson.

As a result of Racine's decision, the USA-2 team, driven by Jill Bakken, also had to change. With rotating teammates, Bakken picked up Vonetta Flowers as her push-mate. Alabama native Flowers was also a former college track star. Yet the focus remained squarely on Racine and Johnson. Bakken and Flowers were merely an afterthought as far as the international media were concerned.

However, at a routine practice just four days prior to the bobsledding event, Johnson pulled a hamstring. Knowing her teammate would not be at full strength to push her sled, Racine contacted Flowers on the eve of the event, asking her to consider jumping teams and help Racine win the gold medal. Flowers politely

declined the offer. She had come to Salt Lake City
to ride with Bakken, and she couldn't turn her back
on her friend and teammate even if it ended up costing
her the gold medal.

"Jill (Bakken) and I tried to stay out of the soap opera,"
Flowers said. "A lot of people saw us as the other team.
We wanted to come here and prove them wrong."

And they did just that. Bakken and Flowers stunned
the field by winning the first heat by a margin of
0.29 seconds—a huge margin in bobsledding. After
a great run like that, the second run was merely a
formality—stay on the track and the underdogs would
take home the gold.

In the finals, Bakken and Flowers bettered the run of
the German sled by 0.3 seconds and captured the gold,
but they won much more than just a bobsled race.
No other African-American woman had participated
in the Winter Olympics—ever. "My goal was to make
the Summer Olympics," said Flowers, "but there was
a different plan for me."

Pushing a sled on the snow track was a far cry from
the sprints and long jumps Flowers had competed
in all her life, but Olympic bobsledder Bonny Warner
realized that Flowers's speed and power on the track
could explode on the bobsled course, and indeed
they did. Flowers made history as the first African-
American ever to win a gold medal at the Winter
Games. More than that, though, she became a model
of integrity, refusing to sacrifice her honor for what

seemed like a sure chance at victory. In the end,
she won both the medal and the admiration of a nation
for her character.

"What can I say?" Flowers said in the aftermath.
"This is a dream come true for me."

ALLYSON

Felix

She is a young woman going somewhere fast.

She is Allyson Felix, one of the world's greatest female sprinters. With constant comparisons to the greats of other eras, she continues to run past every current opponent in the world on her way to virtual dominance of her generation.

"Allyson didn't run track until ninth grade," said her father, Paul Felix. "That was the first time she put on track shoes."

Allyson's mother, Marlean, recalled the day Allyson tried out for the track team. "The coach thought his stopwatch was broken, so he had to go back and have her try again. I think she was running in these big basketball shoes, but he pointed out that she was just so quick."

When Allyson was in the ninth grade, she made it to the California high school state finals. The next year, she won the state title in the 100 meters. And by her senior year, she was running with some of the world's elite athletes.

"She's 17 and she's running against some 25-year-olds," said Marlean. "For track and field, 24, 25 seem to be the prime for women, and here she was beating them."

At 18, Allyson stunned the track-and-field world by running to a silver medal in the 200 meters at the 2004 Olympics in Athens. She also broke the world junior record in the event. A year later, she won the world championship. It was clear that the teen from California had arrived.

As she watched her daughter receive her medal at the Olympics, Marlean had flashes of Allyson on the track. "When they put that wreath on her head and when they hung that medal around her neck, it all came together—

all that she had gone through to reach this point at such a tender age. The emotions just overtook me."

"I felt really proud just receiving my medal," said Allyson. "When I initially finished the race I was disappointed, but my family helped me put everything into perspective, and I was able to see what I had accomplished and see the amount of time it took."

She would experience that sense of momentary disappointment again, but not often. Her world championship run lasted through 2007, and in 2008, she was again the silver medalist in the 200 meters at the Olympic Games in Beijing, China. Though the gold eluded her grasp once again, Allyson remained gracious and humble.

Much of Allyson's humility comes through the support of her own family. Her father has been a great mentor to Allyson. Her brother, Wes, has been part training partner and part cheerleader. "We've tried to train her not to bring the attention to herself," said Paul. "Very rarely will she show emotion when she wins a race. She'll never be the kind of individual who pumps up her hand with number one or anything like that."

"Everyone is always watching you and everything that you do," said Allyson, "so I feel like that's your best opportunity to really show what you're about."

The world watched as the Felix family surrounded a disappointed Allyson following her second-place finish in the 200-meter run in Beijing. Her family lifted her spirits by reminding her of what she had just accomplished and helped her gain perspective.

As part of that perspective, Allyson decided to take part in a new drug-testing program in the summer of 2008. Tired of the proverbial black cloud that performance-enhancing drugs cast over the U.S. track-and-field program, Felix fought her own public war, submitting to a significant number of random tests, which were both uncomfortable and inconvenient. Allyson knew that her actions could help restore credibility to the sport and allow her to demonstrate the values her family instilled in her and which she has based her life upon.

"Whatever I can do to prove I'm clean, no matter what time I have to wake up or where I have to drive, I'm willing," Felix, the world champion in the 200 meters, told the *Los Angeles Times.* "I feel more responsible myself to be a role model for younger kids . . . that's important to me. I'm trying to make a name for myself, and after I run, I hope that people can distinguish my character and the way I present myself, so that's what I am really striving for."

CYNTHIA
Cooper

As the first-ever star of women's professional basketball in America, Cynthia Cooper was an anomaly. She was gracious and austere off the court, but intense and driven when playing. At 37, she would seem to have been an athlete past her prime, yet at that age she finished her career in 2000, maintaining her role as the most dominant player in the WNBA and leading her team to an unprecedented fourth consecutive championship.

Cooper was the league's first superstar and MVP during each of its first two seasons. She led the Houston Comets to the league title in each of the league's first four years of existence, 1997-2000. And when she retired following the 2000 season, she did so fulfilled in knowing she was the one person most responsible for giving the fledgling league a solid identity right from the get-go.

But while Cooper was dazzling fans on the court night in and night out, her insides were churning as she walked through intense personal tragedy. Her smile and pleasant nature belied the burdens she carried while lifting her sport to professional acceptance.

Those close to her know, however, what Cooper has had to endure. They saw it when she affixed a pink ribbon to her uniform to signify her support for breast cancer research. They saw it when she used to hurry into the Houston locker room after each road game to call her mother, Mary Cobbs, who eventually died from the disease in 1999. They saw it when Comets coach Van Chancellor moved practice back by half an hour once in a while so Cooper had time to take her mom for another battery of tests or a chemotherapy treatment session. They saw it when Cooper wistfully looked at photos or the jersey of former teammate, roommate, and close friend Kim Perrot, who died of cancer in 1999.

After all, it was Perrot herself who used to stay up late at night with Cooper when the team was on the road, talking about holding on to hope and why bad things happened to good people.

Being on the court seemed to be a relief for Cooper. She was a pure scorer who exuded an "I dare you to stop me" attitude. The league's all-time scoring leader, she was equally as comfortable draining a jumper in a defender's face as she was whisking by her on the way to the hoop.

While she was vivacious on the court, Cooper tended to be stoic about herself and her off-the-court challenges. She would not easily volunteer information regarding the emotions she struggled with or how she went to the aid of both her mother and Perrot. Few know, for example, that Cynthia escorted her mom through every stage of her cancer treatment in '97. Or that she frequently stayed up until 3 a.m. to do the ironing and other household chores for her mother. Nor do many know that she has helped raise a niece and nephew and has adopted another nephew, Tyquon. All together, she now has five nieces and nephews who live with her.

For Cooper, playing through a hamstring pull or ankle sprain was minimal in comparison to what her mother endured or what Perrot went through.

Mary Cobbs learned she had breast cancer just weeks after she and her daughter received the joyful news that the WNBA had assigned Cooper to play in Houston, the family's adopted hometown. At least there, Cooper thought, she would be home enough to help care for her mother.

"It was unbelievable how it all worked out," Cooper said.

While the WNBA was marketed as the game that would be ruled by such media darlings as Lisa Leslie and Rebecca Lobo, it was Cooper who took the league by storm. The 5-foot-10-inch shooting guard displayed her all-around game and for four years outplayed the others, quickly setting the league's single-game scoring record with 44 points only 10 games into the season.

"She's the best all-around player I've ever faced," said New York Liberty guard Vickie Johnson.

Her success in the WNBA was a far cry from the tears she shed as a youngster. Cooper spent her teenage years in a crime-ridden neighborhood in the Watts section of Los Angeles. Her mother made significant sacrifices to raise Cynthia and her seven siblings. Sports became a way out of the pain of a childhood partially lost. Even then, Cooper's basketball career didn't begin until she was 16, and then it was only accidental.

She may have picked up basketball by accident, but she rode the wave it provided to a great career. She played on the '83 and '84 NCAA championship teams at USC. She was a member of two U.S. Olympic teams, earning a gold medal at the '88 games in Seoul, South Korea,

and a bronze at Barcelona in '92. Still, she never felt
completely challenged to utilize all of her talents.

The evolution of her game began during her 11 seasons
as a pro in Europe, beginning in 1986.

She became that superstar type of player with the teams
Alcamo and Parma in the Italian league. In the 1995-96
season, Cooper averaged 35.5 points per game for
Alcamo. She arrived in the WNBA as a full-fledged,
known scorer. To become such, her work regimen
at times included firing up to 300-500 shots per day
in practice. And it all paid off.

In the first WNBA season, Cooper led the league
in scoring at 22.2 per game and was also selected as
the title game MVP after a 25-point effort. She began
to receive endorsement offers and show up on talk
shows and in WNBA promotional spots. She was now
the league's true marquee player, much like those she
had grown accustomed to playing caddie to years before.

In the aftermath of that first glorious season, Cooper
would say it was all the more sweet for her in that she was
able to share it with her mother.

In '98, she repeated her performance in a nearly
identical fashion, scoring 22.7 points per game to lead
the league—and again leading her team to the title and
a 27-3 regular season record.

But 1999 would provide the biggest challenge yet. There
were the expectations to win a third consecutive title,
but other burdens grew heavier.

Cooper turned in her third straight outstanding performance on the court—and in the finals—and again led the league in scoring at 22.1 points per game while also leading in assists at 5.7 per game. But in the midst of her continuing excellence, she faced her most difficult defeats.

On February 12, 1999, Cooper's mother lost her battle with breast cancer. Ten days later, Perrot was diagnosed with lung cancer that had spread to her brain. In six months, Cooper's close friend was dead at the age of 32. Following the '99 finals win, Cooper stood atop the media table near center court and held aloft Perrot's jersey as if to tell the world she and her teammates had won it all for their fallen friend. It was a victory she seemed to will herself and her team to.

"She's got the greatest will to win of any player I've ever seen, man or woman," said former coach Chancellor. "I've heard a lot about Larry [Bird], Magic [Johnson], and Michael [Jordan] having the greatest will to win, but I'm going to put Cynthia Cooper up there against anybody."

Cooper finished her wondrous basketball tour with a fourth straight WBNA title and fourth straight finals MVP award in 2000. Then she simply walked away from the game the same way she first entered—with grace, class, and composure, and as a model of how to prioritize one's life.

BETSY

King

Betsy King is one of the most successful women's professional golfers on the planet.

However, she's more than just a golfer. She is also a compassionate humanitarian. When the topic turns from golf to people—particularly people in need—passion is ignited in Betsy King.

In 1993, just two days after birdieing the final hole of the last tournament of the season to lock up her third LPGA Player of the Year title, King was surrounded by Romanian street children. "I went from celebrating an incredible win and season to extreme sadness," said King. "I was so happy, and then it all became very, very clear. I said to myself, 'How important is golf, anyway?' We were standing in the snow, freezing, dealing with young children who live under a train station. It gave me a perspective that has changed my life."

So after a whirlwind week in mid-November of '93—King won the Toray Japan Queens Cup in Kobi, Japan, then took a red-eye flight to Arizona, where she spent a day at home in Scottsdale unpacking and packing—King and four fellow LPGA players hopped on a plane for Bucharest to work with an orphan-relief group called Extended Hand of Romania.

 King and her golfing partners experienced the desolate living conditions in Romania. During their trip, they stayed with a family who had no indoor plumbing. King and Alison Nicholas were so moved by the family's plight that they financed the installation of indoor plumbing.

"We experienced firsthand what it was like to live without the basic necessities that we take for granted," King said. "Their home was barely heated, but in spite of their poverty, they gave us everything they had. We ate all the time, it seemed. They were so strong that it made me even stronger."

King and her friends had come to help, so they went about their weeklong mission, visiting several orphanages scattered throughout three cities, delivering food, clothing, and medicine, and extending love and hugs. The experience left an indelible impression on the entire group. In 1994, they returned to Romania to again provide basic needs to more orphaned children.

King remembers a particular moment from her Romanian adventure that seemed to crystallize the entire experience. Her group located a five-year-old boy named Daniel who was being adopted by a family in the Seattle area. The golfers picked up Daniel from an orphanage and dressed him in a new outfit provided by his adoptive parents. Daniel stayed with King and the others throughout their trip, becoming so attached that he cried when they said their good-byes in Bucharest prior to the boy's flight to the U.S.

"He is one of the lucky ones," King said. "It was wonderful to be able to help make things better for him. The whole country is so poor. It's sad to think about the children we left behind."

King's commitment to those who have been left behind extends beyond Romania. She has spent time in Korea, using golf as a tool for aid work. And each off-season for the past several years, she has helped out on domestic soil as well.

King has been involved in annual projects with Habitat for Humanity. Each year in mid-October, following the end of the Tour's domestic season, she puts down her clubs for a week and picks up saws, hammers, nail guns, and tool belts, building houses for poor families in various parts of the country for a couple weeks of hard labor, meager accommodations, and building hope.

"We believe you're called to serve others," said King, who has spearheaded the project that has seen as many as 30 golfers involved at one time. "We have made a difference, I think. Obviously, you don't change the world, but you try to change the world you're in."

"I've never met someone with a servant attitude like hers who wants to learn more and grow," said John Dolaghan, Director of Golf for FCA and a friend of King's. "She's as authentic as they come."

Said Bill Lewis, a retired U.S. Navy captain who worked on the LPGA circuit for a number of years, "I've never met a superstar athlete with so much humility."

"There is always a need, but you can't do everything," said King. "How can I help? All I can do is live one day at a time and do things with all my heart."

CAT

Whitehill

Considered one of the finest players on the planet, Cat Whitehill burst onto the soccer scene after learning the sport in Birmingham, Alabama—a place not exactly known as the soccer capital of the world. She led her high school team to four championships and scored a state record seventy-eight goals in her second season.

Whitehill went on to play for the most prestigious soccer program in the country at the University of North Carolina. As a Tar Heel, she needed some gentle guidance, and she found a true mentor in her coach, Anson Dorrance.

"When I was younger I made most every team and I started for most of those teams," she said. "I definitely struggled with starting and not starting with those teams, but not to the extreme of what happened to me when I came to North Carolina."

"Cat knew that she didn't work hard enough during the summer and didn't earn the right to play," said Dorrance. "She played every game off the bench and that was really hard for a player of her level to accept."

"I came in expecting to start," Whitehill reiterated. "It turns out I was not brought up like I should have been in the soccer world. I came in kind of naïve and didn't come in as fit as I should or even technically as good as I should have."

Dorrance's techniques worked for Whitehill. She eventually became a star at UNC and made All-America teams. In 2003, she led the Tar Heels to the NCAA title, earning the college player-of-the-year honors. She then made her mark on the global stage, becoming one of the leading scorers for the 2003 U.S. Women's World Cup Team. Later, she helped Team USA win the gold at the 2004 Summer Olympics.

"Playing for [Coach Dorrance]—it is the reason why I am sitting here today," said Whitehill. "I would not have made the national team if it was not for his always beating on me to be the better player. And I am so thankful that I got to play with him."

"Here she goes from our bench to starting for the U.S. Women's National Team, and that's extraordinary," said Dorrance.

"When you make that team and you get to play with people like Mia Hamm and Julie Foudy, it is the ultimate experience," Whitehill concurred.

Whitehill's rise to the top, while unusually quick, is not surprising given her approach. In a day of pampered celebrity athletes, her continuing willingness to yield to the authority of her coaches has helped set her apart. Yet taking this posture is nothing new for Whitehill.

"Here she is with an Olympic gold medal, and she's been on all the national teams in women's soccer, and you would think that everything is handed to her on a silver platter, but all along the way there have been those hard times, those little things that make you a better person," said Whitehill's mother, Anne Reddick. "Instead of letting that defeat her or discourage her, she took that as a challenge and pushed forward."

"I have been brought up in an incredible family where they've taught me that humility is the key to everything," said Whitehill. "Because if you are humble to anyone, then you gain respect that way . . . . I think earning respect is a huge part of becoming a better person."

"All of her teammates think the world of her, not just because of her athleticism . . . but she doesn't wear that off the field—she's a very sweet kid, she cares about her teammates," Dorrance said.

Perhaps even more impressive is Whitehill's passion for equality. An advocate for the rights of women to participate in sports, Whitehill testified in front of a U.S. Senate committee in support of Title IX, the civil rights law that guarantees women and girls are given the same opportunities to participate in school sports that men and boys are offered. She described how she had to play on boys' soccer teams when she was growing up because there were no girls' teams in her area at the time.

An incredible soccer player, Cat Whitehill has accomplished great things. But, she said, it was "Title IX [that] gave me the true opportunity to live my dream."

ALEX

Scott

Alexandra Scott was a little girl with a big dream. And she proved that when little steps come with big effort, the biggest of dreams can come true—and the resulting impact can be huge.

In 2000, four-year-old cancer patient Alex Scott committed herself to a seemingly simple idea—sell lemonade to help her doctors find a cure for childhood cancer.

"Alex was smart; she developed a plan," said her mother, Liz Scott. "She would sell lemonade from a lemonade stand. Keeping the money was not in her mind. She would give it to her hospital for the cure they would find."

Alex exhibited this type of determination her entire life. Shortly before her first birthday, she was diagnosed with neuroblastoma, a common type of childhood cancer. Doctors said that if she beat the cancer, it was doubtful that Alex would ever walk again. Just two weeks later, though, Alex slightly moved one leg at her parents' request. It was a clear indicator of who she would turn out to be—a courageous and inspiring child who believed in big dreams.

By her second birthday, Alex was crawling and able to stand up with leg braces. She gained strength and learned how to walk. She appeared to be beating the disease, but the following year, doctors made the heartbreaking discovery that her tumors were growing again.

In 2000, Alex received a stem cell transplant. While recovering in the hospital, she told her mother about her idea for the lemonade stand.

With the help of her older brother, Patrick, Alex set up the first Alex's Lemonade Stand for Childhood Cancer on the family's front lawn that July. That first year she raised $2,000 for "her hospital."

She continued her business venture, and by 2002, Alex's Lemonade Stand had attracted significant media attention. Her story was featured on *Oprah*, *The Today Show*, *The CBS Early Show*, *The CBS Evening News*, CNN, MSNBC, Fox News, and dozens of other news segments across the country. Her story was told in *People Magazine*, *Sports Illustrated*, *Good Housekeeping*, *USA Today*, and hundreds of other newspapers and magazines worldwide. She was recognized by various news organizations as one of the top 10 people of the year, and *USA Today* named her one of the 21 worldwide figures whose lives affected news, entertainment, sports, and business in 2004.

"I told her if she raised three or four thousand dollars, that would be a lot, and two thousand would be fine, too," said Liz. "She said she thought she would raise more than that."

And Alex did just that. While persevering through six operations and countless other treatments in fewer than three years, Alex sold a lot of lemonade. She reported making $12,000 in just one day. Her ultimate goal: to raise a million dollars for pediatric cancer research.

Despite her deteriorating health, Alex held her annual lemonade stand through 2004. As news spread of this remarkable sick child who was dedicated to helping other sick children, people from all over the world were moved by her story and followed her inspirational example.

Thousands of lemonade stands and other fund-raising events began to be held across the country by children, schools, businesses, and organizations—all to benefit Alex's Lemonade Stand Foundation for Childhood Cancer. Alex's Lemonade Stands would be found in all fifty states, as well as in Canada and France.

On August 1st, 2004, Alex lost her battle with cancer. She died peacefully at the age of eight after fulfilling her dream to raise $1 million to help find a cure for the disease that took her life.

"What she has done and what she has accomplished in her life still amazes me, and I am so proud," said Liz. "She was a girl who wanted all the same things other girls want, but she couldn't have them and she made the best of what she could have and then some."

Alex's story has inspired thousands of people from all walks of life to raise money and give to her cause. Today her legacy lives on through the Alex's Lemonade Stand Foundation for Childhood Cancer. To date, there are more than 8000 Alex's Lemonade Stands across the world, and the foundation has raised more than $20 million for childhood cancer research.

And just think—it all started with one special little girl's commitment to make a difference with a simple glass of lemonade.

AMELIA

Landreth

For Amelia Landreth, it was clearly an unfair situation.

The boys' basketball team at Crenshaw High School in California was sponsored by Nike and decked out in great uniforms, sweats, and shoes. But Amelia's girls' team had tattered uniforms that looked like they came straight from a thrift shop. While she considered the situation an injustice, Amelia recognized that either no one noticed, no one cared, or no one had the courage to do anything about it—except her.

It can be difficult to persuade anyone to part with money for just one item. But to convince people to donate money to an entire team of high school girls seemed far more difficult. That is, to everyone but Amelia.

In 2002, the 17-year-old junior at Crenshaw came up with a plan to outfit her teammates in better style. After all, she reasoned, how would the team learn to play like winners if they never looked like winners?

Amelia set out on a mission to pound the pavement in search of a company, a person, or anyone who would fund her team's uniform needs. One 17-year-old girl busting the streets of the Watts section of L.A. to find a sponsor during a slumping economy is a long shot at best. But then, the junior varsity guard always had been a pretty good shot.

She knocked on doors, rang telephones, and pestered people, relentless in her quest. Feeling a responsibility to her team, her school, and herself, Amelia was determined to work her neighborhood until she came back with the answer she wanted.

"I just couldn't believe that the boys' team had sponsorship and the girls' didn't," Amelia said.

Amelia's business plan was structured and sound. She included projected expenses and talked at length about the value to the school, the community, and to the individual players. "My proposal included an outline of our traveling expenses and the cost of uniforms and shoes," Amelia said.

When it seemed her plan might fail, Amelia pressed on and found another way.

"I searched the yellow pages and started picking up business newsletters, and that's how I found out about Roscoe's Chicken & Waffles," she said.

Roscoe's Chicken & Waffles is something of a landmark in South Central Los Angeles. The longtime favored restaurant has five locations in the area, including one right near Crenshaw High. The owners of this establishment that has served entertainers, athletes, and lawmakers have a heart for the area, so they responded to Amelia's pleas. Roscoe's stepped up with the majority of the funding and became the team's sponsor. But not before Amelia had had her fill of denials.

"I got a lot of rejections," Amelia said. "But I didn't give up. I didn't ever give up."

Amelia negotiated over $5000 in sponsorships for both the varsity and junior varsity teams. She later received a $5000 matching donation from the Miller

Foundation. She had been persuasive in her pitch, and the people responded.

"When talking to people, you have to be honest, straightforward, and to the point," she said. "I got a lot of rejection, but that didn't stop me."

For her tireless efforts to give back to her team and school, Amelia was honored with a special commendation presented at a ceremony by the Los Angeles County Board of Supervisors. More important, she won admiration and respect from her teammates, friends, and the entire school.

ANDREA

Jaeger

Andrea Jaeger understands what it means to be a child of isolation. A tennis prodigy who became the second-ranked player in the world in 1979 at the age of 14, the Chicago native was America's great hope for tennis domination. Yet she felt alone. So today, while many of those she played against are still swinging their rackets to make millions, Jaeger is out asking for money to help children in need.

Jaeger started playing tennis when she was eight. By 14, she had scored victories over such luminaries as Chris Evert and Martina Navratilova. When a shoulder injury ended her career at 19, she saw it as a new beginning. The once-shy teen who captivated fans around the world with her long pigtails, braces, and strong forehand is now an outgoing champion for kids—a cause to which she has dedicated her life.

In 1990, Jaeger founded the Silver Lining Foundation for children with cancer in Aspen, Colorado. She used her $1.4 million in tennis earnings to launch the foundation, in an effort to make life better for terminally ill kids. Young cancer patients are flown to Aspen for a week of support and activities, such as horseback riding and whitewater rafting.

She reaches out to kids because she cares and because she can relate. Her early fame isolated her from peers at school, and her age alienated her from other pro tennis players.

"The other kids had a very difficult time," Jaeger said. "They resented [me] and threw food at me in the lunchroom and pushed me into lockers. It wasn't a fun time to grow up."

Out of those experiences birthed a heart of compassion for kids in need. It came to fruition one day on the way back from a tennis match in New Jersey in 1980. Jaeger, then 15, was overtaken with a sudden conviction to help sick children. She told the driver of her limo to stop at a toy store, where she bought several hundred dollars' worth of gifts to give to kids in the critical-care unit of Helen Hayes Hospital in West Haverstraw, New York.

"I just felt a calling at that moment," said Jaeger.

As she continued on the pro tennis circuit, her compulsion to help grew. Jaeger often surprised hospitalized children with presents, as she had done that first day. She wanted them to know someone cared. Each opportunity to touch a child's life made her compassion burn stronger.

For two years as she worked to create the foundation, Jaeger took a job as an airline ticket agent, using the flying benefits to conduct research, raise funds, and visit children. Several tennis players contributed to the foundation. Then a couple donated 10 acres of land, and a businessman gave $1.7 million to build the 18,000-square-foot facility Jaeger now oversees. At the facility, all programs are customized so each child can participate and each can experience the simple joys of being a child.

"They get to abandon being treated like a sick person," said Jennifer Boisture, a volunteer with the foundation. "There, having cancer is normal. The children really bloom."

"Andrea does this for all the right reasons and it shines through her actions," said model Cindy Crawford, who, with other sports and entertainment celebrities, participates in hands-on foundation activities with the kids. "She is utterly selfless and completely devoted to helping others."

Jaeger divides her time between being hands-on with the kids and raising over $2 million in donations each year for the foundation's operations. She also underwrites reunions, family retreats, college scholarships, internships, and programs that come to children who can't travel because of their illnesses. It is her passion to spread compassion to these children.

"My family and friends were so upset when I got injured, but I knew in my heart that I was called to help kids," she said. "Everyone could use someone who cares."

ANN

Fudge

Ann Fudge is one of the top leaders in today's business world. Her meteoric rise through the ranks of corporate power has made her one of the most influential decision-making women in American business. Yet her success has gone relatively unnoticed by most media outlets.

Fudge made history in 2003 when she became the first African-American female to be named CEO of a major company. Fudge was appointed as chairwoman and chief executive officer of Young & Rubicam, Inc., a major division of a global advertising agency, the WPP Group. With the historic announcement, Fudge also became the chief executive officer of the largest unit of Y&R, Young & Rubicam Advertising, which creates campaigns for such top brands as AT&T, Colgate, Dr Pepper, Lincoln, and Sears. The appointments also made Fudge one of the few African-American chief executives in the United States.

Fudge's achievement is all the more impressive because of what she has had to overcome. Said *New York Times* reporter Judith H. Dobrzynski of Fudge: "She had to crash through not merely the glass ceiling that stymies white women, but an all-but-insurmountable 'concrete wall' that researchers say blocks blacks and other minorities from companies' upper echelons."

As a teenager, Fudge witnessed the urban riots in the wake of Martin Luther King, Jr.'s assassination in 1968 and said those experiences helped her gain focus.

"They made me incredibly determined," she said in a *New York Times* interview. "I wanted to do something that black people hadn't done before. When I hit roadblocks, that was what kept me going."

Later, while a student at Simmons College, Fudge met Margaret Henning, author of *The Managerial Woman*, who told Fudge that she recognized in her some of the skills crucial to becoming a corporate executive. Henning encouraged Fudge to pursue it as a career.

Following a business degree from Simmons and an MBA from Harvard Business School, Fudge was hired by General Mills, where she immediately set a timetable of professional goals, including becoming the general manager of a brand by the age of 40.

She quickly moved up the corporate ranks and, in 1983, became director of marketing, responsible for four brands. Her team developed and introduced Honey Nut Cheerios, which quickly became one of the division's top performers.

In 1986, Fudge accepted an offer from Kraft Foods, the nation's largest consumables manufacturer, in order to be close to her ailing mother. As brand manager there, Fudge was responsible for part of a $2 billion advertising budget and had dramatic successes.

"As a business leader, Ann combines a very forceful personality with a great sensitivity to people," her former boss at Kraft, Robert S. Morrison, said. "She relies heavily on a team approach to achieving business goals."

In 1991, Fudge was promoted to general manager of the brand division, a year ahead of the goal she had set. She was also named executive vice president at Kraft and was responsible for the success of well-known brands such as Grape Nuts, Kool Aid, Jell-O, and Altoids. In 1998, she was named by *Fortune* magazine as one of the 50 most powerful women in American business.

Throughout her rise to the top, Fudge refused to compromise her values, once turning down a top job offer that required a move to another city. "It would have meant relocating just as my son was entering his senior year in high school," she said. "I didn't think it would be right to move him that year. And I did not want to be a commuter wife and mom."

Fudge's astounding success and business demeanor attracted attention from the nation's top corporate heads and led to her historic hiring at Young & Rubicam. Those who know her know she is the perfect person for the unprecedented title. As a colleague of hers once said, "She's eminently qualified and a terrific leader."

Fudge said there are no hidden formulas to her leadership success. Rather, she said it is all about relating to people. "I lead from a core of integrity, honesty, and respect for the individual. I'm open and I listen. The ability to truly listen to all perspectives is the key to real leadership. Then acting decisively, and many times courageously, even if my perspective is not aligned with the group—this is the true test of leadership."

BEV

Kearney

As the University of Texas women's track coach, it seemed that Beverly Kearney's entire professional career was about speed.

But when she was ejected from an SUV when the driver lost control and crossed the median on Florida's Interstate 10, everything changed. Now, it is all about strength—the kind that comes from deep within. Now, even when Bev Kearney's body is not willing, her heart still is.

Kearney sustained a serious spinal cord injury that left her unable to walk. "I was in the hospital laughing and joking, not knowing I had a huge bandage on my head with staples in my scalp and scars all over my face," she said. "As I became more aware, I didn't want to see myself that way. I refused to see myself as a [paraplegic]."

Three surgeries realigned several vertebrae along her spine. She needed extensive rehabilitation to regain the lost feeling and motion in her lower extremities. Over the following months, Kearney slowly gained feeling and she began to stand briefly with the aid of supports or crutches. Before long, she was able to use a walker, making rapid progress that exceeded expectations.

Doctors said Kearney survived because she was in tremendous physical condition and had an indomitable will to win. In short, Kearney's a survivor.

Prior to the accident, the seven-time national coach of the year led Texas to four NCAA national championships and 13 league titles since she arrived in Austin in 1993. While her team's accomplishments are impressive, it is her ongoing and positive impact on the lives of student athletes that has transcended the sport.

Her program was built on a family atmosphere, and her players are known for their teamwork and determination. Kearney instilled her iron will and indomitable spirit in her teams. It is that depth of character that pushed her on the road to recovery.

"She has done so much for athletics at Texas, and through all of this, she has shown the fight and courage to battle against a lot of tough obstacles," said U.T. football coach Mack Brown. "We appreciate her great spirit."

Even during her recovery, Kearney was determined to motivate her team. While in rehab, she watched videotapes of practices and meets and drew up workouts for the squad, even though she could not be there. Within four months of the accident, she was attending practice almost every day. She coached her athletes with the same intensity as before. She refused to let her team down because of her circumstances.

"I tell them, 'Your gifts haven't been lessened by my injury, your opportunities haven't been lessened by my injury. Don't use me as an excuse for failure,'" Kearney said.

Kearney admitted she struggled at times with the reality of being forced to use a wheelchair. But she said she has cried more often filled with the joy brought by well-wishers' hundreds of e-mails, cards, and letters—many from people she did not know—and phone calls, including one from President Bush. "I've just been overwhelmed with all the support," she said.

Kearney had to come to terms with the reality of what a full recovery demanded—perhaps years of rehabilitation—yet she wasn't about to give up.

"This isn't something I would wish on my worst enemy," Kearney said. "It's just something in my life that I have to go through . . . . I don't feel sorry for myself."

Kearney's moment in the sun came at the Texas Relays, just four months after her accident. With a large crowd looking on, she stood for the first time in public, realizing a dream she had had five weeks earlier and a promise she had made to those around her. It may have appeared to be just a 30-second moment in time, but it was a display of strength and perseverance for the ages.

"Everybody thought I was crazy, and everybody said there was no way," she said of the inspiring moment. "My muscles had gone into atrophy, and I couldn't even move my own leg. I was in a very weak spot with my spine, and to say you will do something of that magnitude, you go on faith. But I knew it would be true. I'm [going to be] walking. I'll probably be jogging. I'm gonna be 100 percent. I have absolutely no doubt . . . . It doesn't matter what anybody else says. I told them, 'Don't get too comfortable with this wheelchair, because it's temporary. I'm walking up out of here one day.'"

BRITTANY

Deyan

Brittany Deyan was like most kids her age. A senior in high school, Brittany was mostly concerned with homework, boys, and things of here and now. Thoughts of there and then never crossed her mind.

Then, in 2006, she watched a video in her international relations class at Newport Harbor (Calif) High School that altered her viewpoint and changed her world. The video was on Invisible Children, a movement designed to rescue children in Uganda from slavery and poor conditions.

"The people who started it (Invisible Children) aren't a whole lot different from me," Brittany said. "It kind of made me question why I wasn't doing something like that. I had seen many documentaries about Africa, but none that conveyed the sense of hope and a goal for the future. Invisible Children gave the necessary outlet to help.

"After I saw this documentary, it motivated me to get involved. It made me, as a single individual, feel like I could make a difference."

Inspired, Brittany started the Invisible Children's Club at her school. Twelve students attended the first meeting. At the end of a 100-day fund-raising drive—in which over $44,000 was raised—close to 150 students were involved and the whole school knew about the program.

"When the Invisible Children people came to our school for a rally, it was at an optional assembly, which usually means about two hundred people will show up," Brittany said. "We had more than one thousand."

Brittany said students at her school typically don't get involved in causes.

"To be perfectly honest, [the school is] pretty much made up of rich kids from Newport Beach," she said. "To see people from this school get involved was huge, because kids usually get involved only if it affects them. Yet in this organization, chances are we will never meet the people we are helping and never see the effects of our efforts. People really had to be in it for the right reasons."

Newport Harbor was one of 10 high schools that raised significant money for the Invisible Children "Schools for Schools" program. The schools that raised the most funds sent two students overseas to see their money in action, so Brittany spent part of her 2007 summer vacation in Uganda working with representatives of Invisible Children and 11 other high school students. Part of their task was to help rebuild Sacred Heart Secondary School, an all-girls school for which Newport Harbor helped raise funds.

"The cool thing is that we didn't have any big donations," Brittany said. "About 90 percent of our donations were $20 or less."

Through the experience, Brittany felt she had been changed. She said she felt that her perspective was more oriented toward others, and she became less focused on herself. And she said she gained an understanding that reaching out to others in need was not just something to consider; rather, it was part of her responsibility as a human being. A responsibility she feels passionate about.

"I've never felt more passionate about anything quite like this before," she said.

CINDY

Abel-
Sanchez

High school tennis coach Cindy Abel-Sanchez knows all about winning and losing. She has instilled these lessons into her students. Yet now those lessons go a little deeper and take on more meaning.

Cindy is a cancer patient.

While Cindy has experienced great success with her teams, in recent years her focus has turned to teaching life lessons along with ground strokes and serving techniques.

In 2004, Cindy was diagnosed with breast cancer. Thankfully, the mass was detected early, and doctors gave Cindy—a nonsmoker and healthy eater—a good chance for survival. In response, Cindy attacked the disease the way she would dissect an opponent on the court—she was determined to win.

"I was worried," Cindy recalled. "But I'm an optimistic person. I knew I could beat it."

Knowing that a cancer patient in good physical condition is better able to handle the illness, she took immediate action. "I really researched the treatment I was about to begin," Cindy said. "I contracted a personal trainer to help me stay physically active. I researched nutrition to make sure that I would improve my immune system by eating well."

Then there was coaching. Cindy knew that her team depended on her in order to compete and learn on the court, and that in all reality, she needed them, too. Her team was key in helping her focus on the positive and in giving her a sense of purpose.

"Leaving the team had never occurred to me when I received my diagnosis," she said. "I knew that I was strong and healthy. I knew working would keep my spirits up, because I really love my job."

Following her diagnosis, she quickly called a team meeting to inform her players of her situation.

"I was amazed about how calm she was about it," Gemma Espejo, the team's No. 1 player, told the *Dallas Morning News*. "There's no way I could have handled it like that."

"This ordeal made it evident that I truly cared about them by sharing this information with them and that they could count on me to return to them," said Cindy.

At the beginning of 2005, Cindy underwent two surgeries and had radiation treatment and chemotherapy.

"She did it and still maintained her same driven personality," said her husband, Robert.

The high school's athletic and wellness coordinator, Pam DeBorde, admits she, too, was amazed by the way Cindy handled the situation.

"It is every lady's fear," she said. "But she had a plan and she made it work. I tell you, she's my hero."

"My students and parents have shown that they will be there to cheer me on, as I will be there for them," Cindy said. "My students are a great source to force me to stay in the moment, leaving no time to worry about distant fears."

Espejo and the other players say that by watching their coach's example, they've learned more than just tennis.

"Coach has taught us life lessons by the way she has had to overcome the things she has had to go through," Espejo said. "She is an inspiration to all of us."

"I know that the most valuable tool I provide my students is the ability to make good decisions in their lives," countered Cindy. "Tennis is a great vehicle to teach this skill due to the nature of the sport. When you are playing tennis as an amateur, you are expected to be honest in all your line calls, scoring, and general tennis courtesy, since participants do not have full-time referees on the tennis court as they play. My students look to me as their teacher and someone that will hold them accountable for their behavior and performance in tennis and academics. I know they are always watching me to see how I handle all situations."

DIXIE

Allen

Like many others, Dixie Allen spends time speaking at various schools, sharing her personal experiences. Yet, Allen's story is unlike most. She is the victim of sexual assault. And she chooses to share her story so others may not end up being victimized, as she was.

In 1990, Allen was raped by a stranger in her own home. At the hospital where she was treated, she was counseled by a victim's advocacy group called Friends of the Family. As she healed emotionally, Allen set her sights on helping others. She spoke out about her assault and talked to the press about the experience just a year after the incident. That process led Allen to her "career" as a volunteer speaker, and in 1999, she joined the staff of Friends of the Family to speak out against sexual violence.

Allen knows that while she can't change what happened to her, she can use the attack as a means to fight for others. "It really gave me the strength and the courage to talk about it," she said. "It has helped so many people to share my experience that it's just been remarkable."

Allen teaches a class called Expect Respect, which explores dating and violence in relationships. The topics of discussion in Allen's class range from how the media portrays men and women to how to get help if a student has been a victim. Allen recognizes that the issue of sexual assault and sexual violence is an international epidemic, which is why she has chosen to share her painful experience.

"It's made me a lot more aware of some of the desperation some of the kids live with and how difficult it is to function when their home lives are in such turmoil. Some of them are holding the family together; some are parenting their own parents. They have so much on their minds, it's a wonder many of them do anything at all except just exist," said Allen.

A recent study commissioned by Liz Claiborne, Inc. showed that 57 percent of teens know friends or peers who have been physically, sexually, or verbally abused. One in three teens reports knowing a friend who has been physically abused by his or her partner. A 2005 Gallup Youth Survey reported that one in eight 13- to 17-year-olds knows someone in an abusive relationship, and that boys are just as likely to experience physical or emotional violence in a relationship before graduating from high school.

Statistics like these are astounding. "One in five high school relationships will be violent, so these kids see it a lot," said Allen. "One in four women will be sexually violated during her lifetime. For boys it happens before the age of 12."

Allen addresses students as if there are victims in the audience, recognizing that in every class, there is likely to be at least one student who has been a victim of rape or domestic violence.

"If I assume that there are [victims], they would feel a lot more comfortable about approaching me as if that were the case," she said. "I try to empower them to believe in themselves and to speak up. I give them questions and let them answer anonymously. This encourages them to speak out and get help."

Some students who have been victims have spoken to Allen privately about their experiences. Others have gone to counselors or teachers they trust to get help as a result of the class. Either way, Allen feels she has succeeded and believes her trial has given her great purpose.

"I believe that I had the ability to speak publicly, and I never had anything to say until that [the attack] happened," she said. "I had to go through healing to get to that point, and I never doubted it would sometimes be painful when I had to relive it."

DOT
Richardson

On a summer Tuesday in Atlanta in 1996, Dot Richardson celebrated her team's historic accomplishment with the rest of her victorious U.S. women's softball teammates. Team USA had just won the gold medal in the first-ever Olympic women's softball competition.

Less than 48 hours later, Richardson went back to work. At 7 a.m. sharp, the power-hitting shortstop and forerunner of her sport returned to the powers of healing, reporting as scheduled for the morning shift at Los Angeles County-USC Medical Center, where she was completing her residency as an orthopedic surgeon.

She was met with quite a welcoming party, as dozens of her colleagues crowded the medical center's front steps. The USC Marching Band feted her with a fanfare. A dozen roses were pressed into her arms as physicians and nurses waved pom-poms and balloons drifted into the sky—all to celebrate Dot's homecoming.

Richardson had taken a yearlong leave from County-USC to pursue her Olympic dream, with three years remaining in her residency. At the time, County-USC was America's busiest public hospital, a place where knife wounds were nearly as common as sports injuries. A public, county-funded hospital, it was the most critical link in caring for L.A.'s low-income residents.

"Being a surgeon is the ultimate dream," said Dot. "I would trade in my gold medal to do what I do here. That's what it's all about."

To live her dream took remarkable sacrifice and a hefty day planner. While in residency, she often worked

20-hour shifts at the hospital and then went to the softball field to practice. The arduous schedule was worth it for Richardson, who felt she was right where she was supposed to be. "Helping people as a doctor is like receiving a gold medal every day," she said. "Medicine is very fulfilling to me because I am able to help people. And nothing satisfies me more."

Richardson continued to balance both worlds for the next four years and returned to the Olympics in 2004, once again leading her team to the gold medal at the games in Sydney, Australia. She then pursued her medical career full-time.

Doctor Dot is still known as the first woman of softball and remains involved in promoting the sport. Carrying the mantle of both softball superstar and ER surgeon is more than most could handle. But Richardson is a bundle of energy and the perfect spokesperson for the sport. She also has the ideal heart and temperament for her profession. Her commitment to seeing both careers succeed without expense to either makes her admired by all.

"I think it just basically comes down to the love that you have for what you're doing and if you believe in what you are doing," said Richardson. "I have dreamed about both of my careers all my life.

"I just enjoy what I'm doing. I'm living my dreams. I've always dreamed since I was a little girl to represent my country and win a gold medal in the Olympics. I had thought that would never happen. I've dreamed about being able to help people, and I've tried to do that through my whole life. And now through medicine, to give back, I'm living my dream every day."

Through a life devoted to helping others, Doctor Dot continues to make a profound impact. Her advice to young girls is simple: "You will succeed in sports, schoolwork, a career, and anything you do when you try to be the best that you can be."

FALLON
Taylor

At age 7, Fallon Taylor became the youngest person to join the Women's Professional Rodeo Association. At 13, she became the second barrel racer ever to qualify for the National Finals Rodeo, where she placed second. At 16, she began working in New York City as a fashion model. It is not hard to understand why Taylor has been called a child prodigy.

Blessed with both supermodel looks and world-class rodeo riding skills, Fallon Taylor is an anomaly. She is equally comfortable in front of a camera and on the back of a horse. But she had to work hard to get to that place.

Inside the rodeo ring, she is a four-time NFR competitor and Rodeo Houston champion, and her roots go deep. She started racing professionally at the age of 7 and earned her WPRA card at age 9. At 11, she set a record when she turned in a run of 15.71 seconds at Resistol Arena.

By 16, she was a regular competitor on the pro rodeo circuit. By 1998, at the age of 17, she had earned more than $250,000 in her barrel racing career. During her precocious preteen and teenage years, she dominated the sport of barrel racing. So how did she get into barrel racing?

"One day I saw a barrel race on television when I lived in Tampa, Florida, and I just decided that's what I wanted to do," said Taylor. Being homeschooled allowed Taylor to participate in numerous rodeo events during her secondary school years. It also provided opportunities to explore new career possibilities.

Modeling was one opportunity that stood out to Fallon, and when the door opened to pursue a career in the field, she jumped at it. Following the 1998 NFR season, then seventeen-year-old Fallon gave up barrel racing and moved to New York to work as a high-end fashion model.

"I retired my horse and decided to pack up and move to Manhattan," Taylor said. "I really enjoyed it, appearing in all of the big magazines—*Cosmopolitan*, *Mademoiselle*. It was just great."

But in 2004, Taylor moved back to her parents' home in Ponder, Texas, to concentrate on both careers. She continued to model with the Campbell Agency in Dallas while she made a comeback in her sport after six years away. Managing both meant juggling schedules.

"I get up real early in the morning and ride some of the colts we have on the ranch," she said. "Then I come to Dallas during the midmorning and work the rest of the day on a shoot. And then on the weekends, I can come to rodeos in the area."

It was the ultimate dichotomy. Taylor went from photo shoots in which she wore elegant outfits and spent hours getting her hair and makeup done to throwing on jeans and cowboy boots and riding horses inside a smelly arena.

While Taylor had no intentions of returning to the WPRA tour full-time because of the demand for her presence on magazine pages, she was still able to enjoy the best of both worlds.

"I was blessed with a good run in those early years," she said. "It's been a straight uphill climb since then. I have absolutely no regrets. I've really been blessed to have done all of that. Now, I really want to try some other things."

Pursuing both professions was grueling; however, Taylor wouldn't have had it any other way. She was committed to giving her all to make the dual career work. This child prodigy was still making every day count.

"You have to keep trying and stick with it," she said. "Always remember to keep your head up and never quit trying. If you have a problem, find a niche and try everything to solve it . . . . Patience is a virtue. As long as you have patience, it does not matter how old or young you are."

FLORENCIA

Krochik

& ANDREA

Savopolos

In 2000, at Corona del Mar High in Newport Beach, California, classmates put a student in a headlock during gym class one day. The boy choked, passed out, and wound up in the hospital. Students who witnessed the attack did nothing to come to the boy's aid nor said anything about it to administrators.

Unfortunately, violent acts like this have become a major problem on school campuses across the nation—and an underlying code of silence intimidates many into saying or doing nothing. But at Corona del Mar High, two girls decided to do something to change that.

Florencia Krochik and Andrea Savopolos thought that physical violence against other students was not acceptable. They saw it as a huge problem that needed to be addressed.

"In seventh and eighth grades, there's more physical violence—that's bullying," said Andrea. "But when there is something like ignoring someone, that's one of the worst ways to discriminate against someone because they feel like they don't exist, like they don't matter . . . . There's a problem with that. Things like name-calling or ignoring people can lead to bigger crimes and bigger problems.

"Everyone has personal prejudices and biases. When you don't even recognize that there's a problem, when all the kids just kind of don't say anything about it, it's like almost as if everything's OK."

In 2003, the two juniors decided to take action. They started Tolerance Among People, or TAP, at the school. In the club's first year of existence, the two girls gathered

some 120 active participants, most of whom met every
Friday morning to dialogue. TAP sponsored assemblies,
held workshops, invited guest speakers to campus, and
became involved in community activities. Florencia and
Andrea had a twofold purpose for the club. First, they
wanted to encourage their peers to treat one another
with respect. Second, they wanted to get students to stand
up and speak out when acts occurred—something most
students viewed as a social no-no.

"There's peer pressure that says, 'Don't say anything,'"
said Andrea. "But when you break that down and the
peer pressure is in the reverse, and people aren't afraid
of being made fun of for saying something or for saying,
'I'm sorry you felt that way,' then it's an obvious way to
get . . . more people to make a difference."

"When you are a teenager, you're just going through
so many changes, physical and emotional," said Florencia.
"Having a group where you belong is the only thing that
they feel is stable. Going out of that group and reaching
out to someone else is a threat to that stability. There
are very few teenagers that can step out and break that
stability or risk breaking it. I think TAP has kind of
broken that. We have over 100 members and so many kids
are in different groups and they would have never talked
to each other.

"We just want them to embrace this problem and realize
that there's a solution to it. Because society has treated
you badly or because your friend has disappointed you or

because you have been beaten doesn't mean that all of the world doesn't want you."

The efforts of the two girls have been recognized. They were honored by the Violence Prevention Coalition of Orange County with Ambassador of Peace Awards and with Building Bridges Awards from the Orange County Human Relations Commission, as well as with the Promising Practices Citation from the Character Education Partnership. Still, they consider what they have seen happen around them as their greatest reward.

"I think that we have broken some barriers," said Florencia. "You see people speaking out. It doesn't just pass by anymore . . . . If you prevent one incident from occurring, it's all been worth it."

"It spread as an actual idea among the students that it's OK to stand up for something, that it's not a rite of passage that you make fun of others," echoed Andrea. "Students come to a new realization that what they do and say, the smallest things, like a smile in the hallway or just averting your eyes when you walk by someone, how much that affects some students and how much you can really make an impact on others, even without saying anything—positive or negative."

JACKIE

Joyner-Kersee

There are those who saw the way she grew up in East St. Louis that would never have joined the word "success" with the name Jackie Joyner. Today they see a woman who has gracefully overcome hurdles on the track and in life to become the epitome of the American Dream.

Jackie was born on March 3, 1962, to poverty-stricken teenage parents Alfred Joyner, Sr. and Mary Joyner in the depressed inner city of East St. Louis. They often slept in the kitchen because the stove was the only source of heat in the house. Joyner-Kersee remembers times when she wore the same clothes two days in a row and kept her shoes until they fell apart. But she thinks her childhood helped make her tough.

At eleven, she saw someone murdered in front of her home; at twelve, her paternal grandmother was shot and killed; at nineteen, she lost her mom to a sudden attack of meningitis, and later that year, she was diagnosed with asthma. As the victim of such devastating experiences, Joyner-Kersee easily could have gone a different direction in life. But because of strong role models, she beat the ghetto odds to become not only a hometown hero but a role model for the entire world.

Joyner-Kersee's road to athletic stardom began at the age of nine, when she enrolled in a special community track program and discovered running. She wasn't the fastest or best runner, but she tried harder than most of the other kids. Suddenly, at age thirteen, things began to click on the track, and it seemed she had a future.

"When I was nine, I did my first race—a 400-meter—and finished last," she said. "But that taught me I didn't have

to win. I could learn just as much or more from
not winning."

As an African American, she learned at an early age how
to handle racial prejudice. She remembers vividly a 1976
Amateur Athletic Union (AAU) track meet held in Poplar
Bluff, Missouri. She was 14 years old and competing with
the East St. Louis Railers. She landed a winning long
jump in her last turn during the qualifying round, a jump
that should have been long enough to put her in the final
round—but a white official failed to record it.

"As a result, I was out of the competition," she
explained. "At the time, I thought it was a deliberate
oversight. The disappointment was all the more bruising
because I had to finish in one of the top three spots to
advance to the AAU Regional competition and to have
a chance at ultimately competing in the AAU National
meet. When the official told me I'd failed to qualify,
tears welled up in my eyes and my body stiffened."

Her coach stepped in to give Joyner-Kersee a sense
of perspective, saying, "Rather than looking for someone
to blame or to be mad with, let's learn from this."

From that point on, she worked harder on her jumps,
and at the end of each long-jump competition, she
would walk by the judges to make sure they'd recorded
her results. She learned from her mistake, and it never
happened again. Now she double-checks everything,
and her calm demeanor continues to shine, even in
adverse circumstances. The racial incidents of her youth
stung, but they inspired her and set a foundation for her

remarkable competitive drive to exceed the expectations of others and herself.

Much of Joyner-Kersee's drive came from her family. "Mom would always tell me, 'Jackie, no matter what, always strive to be a good person.' From her I learned that whatever you do is a test of character, a test of heart. Will you choose a godly path or your own? That was crucial for me—especially living in the inner city."

At Lincoln High School, Joyner-Kersee was a star basketball player. She also played volleyball and long jumped and became good enough to earn a college scholarship to UCLA, where she became a budding star. She started for the Bruins basketball team all four years, but on the track she began to make her mark as an athlete of elite quality. She set school, state, and national records in the heptathlon and long jump.

Joyner-Kersee's character and talent shone brightest on the biggest of stages. At the summer Olympic Games in '84, '88, '92, and '96, she gained a reputation as the world's greatest female athlete through her record-setting performances in the heptathlon and long jump.

On the track, Joyner-Kersee is focused and serious, but there's another side to her. Her friends say she's strong on the outside but soft on the inside—a warm, funny, generous, and genuinely kind person.

Said Fred Thompson, a coach for the 1988 women's Olympic track team, "I don't know a person in this world who has a negative thing to say about Jackie . . . . She's a lady. And it's not just on her lips—she goes out there and does things."

Part of what she does is reach out to kids. Joyner-Kersee knows young people look up to her, and she feels it's her duty as an Olympic champion to give something back to the community. She has given countless motivational talks at schools and spoken to kids in hospitals and churches. She has donated money to help reopen the Mary Brown Community Center in East St. Louis, where she first learned to run. She has also funded a scholarship to a National Merit Scholar from her old high school, and she's sent teams of children from her old neighborhood to the AAU Junior Olympic Championships. And in addition to all that, she's currently building the Jackie Joyner-Kersee Youth Center in East St. Louis. For her commitment to youth, Washington University in St. Louis granted her an honorary doctor-of-law degree.

She also cares about fighting poverty and homelessness. She provides scholarships through the Jackie Joyner-Kersee Community Foundation and, more important still, puts in time working hands-on with kids in her hometown.

"I like kids to get to know me," Joyner-Kersee said. "Sure, I've achieved a lot, but the thing is to let them see that everyone is raw material. I want to be a good statement of possibilities." She wants to see those kids have the opportunity to achieve greatness, as well as just to have fun. "I find it touching, in a sense, that people want my autograph and they're in tears," she said. "I think, my gosh! I'm just happy that I'm in the position I'm in and that people would even take the time to talk to me.

"I feel that as an African-American woman, the only thing I can do is continue to better myself, continue to perform well . . . . I hope that someone who's watching me is also educating herself about what she can do to be consistent, what she can do to provide a message . . . as I've tried to do."

Joyner-Kersee's humility is real. She doesn't have her Olympic medals on display. She'd rather show off her Barbie doll collection or humanitarian honors.

"I try not to let my athletic accomplishments change who I am inside," she said. "Athletics has given me a great opportunity to be a role model for the world. But what I'm giving back is far more important: I'm showing kids that with determination, courage, and getting on the right track with school . . . they can be successful. I want to cheer them on—to show them there's so much more to life than winning.

"I want to give people the courage and determination to realize they can change their life. But I also tell them, 'Don't follow in my footsteps. Make your own.'"

JANE

Smith

In 2000, Richard and Deborah Evans's son, Michael Carter, was dying. His new middle school science teacher, Jane Smith, decided to save Michael's life.

Michael had suffered from kidney disease since he was 16 months old. As a 14-year-old, he had been waiting for a kidney donor for over a year.

"I was mad because I had to go on a machine that made me sick or it would make me tired," Michael recalled.

The compassionate teacher felt she had the perfect solution.

"He needed a kidney and I had one," Jane said.

Michael was surprised at the offer from his teacher. This wasn't just an extra-credit way to get an A; it was an assist from a new teacher that would save his life.

"It amazed me at first because she just gave me a straight out yes," said Michael.

About a dozen of Michael's friends and relatives had already tried to be donors, but none of their kidneys matched. Jane's did. She understood the gravity of Michael's situation and was moved with compassion. She also was aware that it would not be easy for her.

"It's a serious operation," said Michael's surgeon, Dr. David Gerber. "Kidney transplant has been around for almost 50 years, but it's still a big undertaking."

Still, Jane was undeterred.

"This world has some real dangers, and I think this is a completely acceptable risk," she said.

"She's a guardian angel," said Deborah Evans of the woman who saved her son's life.

"I want to see Michael when he graduates from college," said Jane. "I want to see him get married and I want to hold his child."

Because of her sacrifice, Jane Smith will have that chance. Michael will be given the opportunity to experience his future. Still, if faced with the same decision again, Jane Smith said she would give the same response.

"The lesson is: Be open to the needs that are in front of you and the riches will come back more than you can imagine," she said.

The future belongs to those
who believe in the beauty
of their dreams.

Eleanor Roosevelt

KAYLA

Burt

Everyone looks for a team to get behind—a group that knows how to work together and epitomizes team spirit. To find this kind of team, one need look no further than the 2002 University of Washington women's basketball team. Not only did the Huskies have a great season on the court, but they did something far more important—they saved the life of a teammate.

Sophomore guard Kayla Burt spent New Year's Eve with five of her teammates. They planned on watching movies and eating pizza together to celebrate New Year's, knowing they had practice at 8:30 the next morning. But an evening of laughter suddenly turned somber. Twenty-year-old Burt began complaining of light-headedness. Moments later, she rolled off the bed and fell face-first to the floor, unconscious.

"We looked at her and it was obvious she wasn't joking around," teammate Giuliana Mendiola said. "We thought she might be having a seizure. We called 911. We slapped her face to wake her up. We kept saying her name to get a response. We rolled her over and she was blue, and it was obvious she needed oxygen."

Kayla's heart had stopped. Over the next several minutes, her five teammates worked to keep her alive. The women didn't know how to perform CPR, but they had seen it enough on TV and in movies to get a vague idea of what to do. Loree Payne and Nicole Castro cleared furniture to give the team room to work. Giuliana pumped Kayla's chest while her sister, Gio, began mouth-to-mouth resuscitation, breathing life back into her teammate.

Erica Schelly relayed CPR instructions from the Medic One operator on the telephone.

Said Gio Mendiola, "Knowing my teammate needed help, I wasn't just going to sit there and freak out. I had to do something."

Paramedics arrived within five minutes of the 911 call—a five minutes, Loree said, that "seemed like an eternity." The medics used electric paddles to revive Kayla, then rushed her to the hospital, with her teammates close behind. The team spent the rest of the night and most of New Year's Day in the hospital together, praying and waiting.

They stayed in the intensive care unit with Kayla until they knew she was out of danger. Incredibly, 2003 began with very good news for Kayla Burt and her teammates— she'd made it.

"They saved my daughter's life," Kayla's mother, Terri, said of the five teammates.

Kayla had suffered cardiac arrest brought on by a rare, previously undiagnosed heart condition called Long QT Syndrome. At one point, she was clinically dead, and if not for her teammates, she would have stayed that way. After Burt endured six days in the ICU, surgeons implanted an electronic defibrillator into her chest that will help her live a normal life. Then they told her that her basketball career was over.

But after serving as a student assistant for her team for a year and a half, Kayla was itching to get back on the court. During her time away from basketball, she visited the Mayo Clinic in Minnesota in an attempt to better understand Long QT Syndrome. There she was told she did not have the heart condition, which opened the door to the possibility of returning to basketball. Over the next few months, she talked with her parents, consulted doctors, and underwent numerous tests. In 2004, she was granted permission by the University of Washington to rejoin her team.

Amazingly, Kayla returned to the court for the 2004-05 season, starting 16 of the team's 29 games. As team captain, she led Washington with 9.6 points and 2.9 assists per game, while ranking second with 1.5 steals per contest.

In 2005, she was named the recipient of the fifth annual V Foundation Comeback Award, given annually by The V Foundation for Cancer Research in collaboration with ESPN. The award is presented to an individual collegiate student-athlete or a team who has accomplished a personal triumph in the face of true adversity, be it in health, life, or moral dilemma. The award is presented in memory of Jim Valvano, the late basketball coach and ESPN commentator whose personal battle with cancer inspired the creation of The V Foundation.

Kayla's remarkable story has a happy ending because of the quick actions of five teammates who have all been profoundly affected by the shared experience.

"She's still with us, you know?" said Gio Mendiola.

Added her sister, Giuliana, "My perspective has changed completely. I always thought basketball was all about winning. But it's really about playing with the people you want to be with and just being together."

"I'm as lucky as anyone has ever been lucky," said Kayla. "They're my sisters for life . . . . We're as close as we can ever be. They gave me CPR. I mean, how much closer can you get?"

"It will always be a part of us," said Loree Payne. "Basically, I saw my best friend in a nonliving condition in her house. She was blue. She was dead. We can play the 'What if?' game. I've done that. Believe me, I've done it a lot and made myself scared. 'What if I had gone downstairs?' 'What if I wasn't there?' But I was there. And there was a reason I was there . . . . Every person had their place and where they needed to be . . . . It shows how important people are in your life."

I never realized until lately
that women were supposed
to be the inferior sex.

Katharine Hepburn

KERRI

Strug

Kerri Strug was the last hope Team USA had for gold in the 1996 Olympic women's team gymnastics competition in Atlanta. To help the U.S. team defeat the dominant Russians, Strug would have to deliver on the vault.

Her first attempt was not good enough. She was a bit off balance leaving the springboard, and she couldn't quite get her body straightened out in the air. The minuscule error in balance resulted in an awkward landing. Her left ankle took the brunt of the impact with the mat. Strug heard a cracking noise, then felt excruciating pain. She knew something was wrong but tried to walk it off. She glanced at the scoreboard. The judges' marks were not enough to push the Americans ahead of the Russians.

So the gymnast faced a decision. She could sit out the next jump and get herself ready for the individual all-around event that would take place the following week—and forfeit her team's chance for gold in the vault competition. Or she could put pain aside and try one more vault, risking severe injury and jeopardizing her shot at individual gold.

Kerri Strug had precious few seconds to decide. With the crowd roaring wildly for her and her ankle throbbing, she made up her mind.

She decided to go for it. Placing her individual opportunity for glory aside, she ran fearlessly toward the vault. She hit the springboard perfectly, thrust herself off the apparatus and into the air . . . and nailed the landing—practically on one leg.

Strug collapsed in pain as her teammates and coaches rushed toward her. As the tears flooded down her cheeks, coach Bela Karolyi picked her up and carried her to the team seating area.

The mark came up. A 9.90 flashed on the scoreboard, meaning Team USA had won the gold medal in the women's team gymnastics competition—for the first time in Olympic history.

Afterward, U.S. team doctors informed Kerri that she had sustained two torn ligaments in her ankle, thus eliminating her from the individual competition. Now she had no chance of achieving an individual gold medal, a dream she had worked at for nearly 15 years.

A coach found her crying over the missed opportunity to compete in the all-around championships and encouraged her by saying, "Kerri, sometimes you don't reach all your goals in life."

But, clearly, Kerri Strug had reached one major goal. In sacrificing her personal dreams for the benefit of the team, she made history by becoming the star of the first-ever American women's gold medal gymnastics team. And she became a true Olympic hero in the process.

KRISTA

Medlock

As a young girl, Krista Medlock never dreamed of being in beauty pageants. She never watched *Miss America* or hoped to someday be on the competitive stage. Then, at 17, she received a recruitment letter from a local pageant, and everything changed.

For the next seven years, pageants were Krista's life. When she wasn't competing, she was coaching. When she wasn't coaching, she was judging. But as she engrossed herself in beauty pageants, she began to notice a change within.

"I loved being in pageants," said Krista, "but at times I didn't really feel comfortable just being me. There's a perception about beauty queens, that they all look a certain way. Even the girls that are in the pageants have to overcome it."

Krista felt pressure to look like the other competitors. She wore more makeup, used hair extensions, and wore a girdle to look as thin as possible.

"Most of the girls would change their hair or go tanning or go on extreme diets," she said. "None of these things are healthy for your body or for your self-esteem. A lot of times I find that girls are getting so caught up in their social circles and what to wear and how to look that they're living in this world where they're floating with no real perception of who they are and what their purpose is," she continued. "That's why they can't make goals for themselves beyond tomorrow. They haven't taken the time to look inside themselves. It's destructive on a lot of levels, but the one that girls really need to understand is that they don't even realize that they're thinking that way. It's about having awareness of why they think the way they think."

At age 23, Krista retired from pageant competition. As she reflected on her experiences, a dream was born. She decided to create a competition that focused more on inner beauty than outer appearance. Her goal was to construct something that helped girls feel good about themselves from the inside out.

Her personal soul-searching led Krista to create the National Distinguished Women's Depth of Beauty pageant. The competition differed from traditional beauty pageants by encouraging participants to display the talent and personality they felt was unique to them and not try to conform to a mold created by others.

"I want to make a statement that it's OK to set your own standard for beauty," she said. "Self-distinction is great. We tell our girls that it's OK to be different. It's a very different statement than they usually get."

The first order of business was to remove the focus on outward appearance. Rather than parading around in swimsuits and evening attire, contestants would be judged on speaking ability and personal style. They would be rewarded for embracing their own unique gifts and abilities.

"When you go into a pageant, you're in a competition to see who the best is," said Krista. "But if you're not striving for your best, what are you getting out of it?"

In the weeks leading up to a pageant, contestants are encouraged to take part in a series of workshops that let them explore their sense of self. They take personality tests and talk about the importance of letting their individual personalities shine through. Krista said that even in a short period of time, she can see a change in how the contestants view themselves.

"Just talking to the girls, you can tell that something has changed," she said. "You can even see it in their posture. Girls are walking with their heads up and their shoulders back. All they needed was to change the way that they saw themselves."

At the first Depth of Beauty pageant, Krista hoped that even a few contestants would show up. She was happily surprised when girls came from all over her state to take part in the event. Today Depth of Beauty has spread to several states, and thousands of young women have participated.

Perhaps no one has learned more through these pageants than Krista herself. These days, she defines beauty much differently than she did during her pageant years. She's realized that true beauty can't be rewarded by a crown or a trophy.

"Knowing who you are and feeling peace about it—that's true beauty," she said.

KRISTINA

Radnoti

California girl Kristina Radnoti has a passion for souls—and soles.

In 2001, at age 17, Kristina began SOLE PURPOSE, a program that donates used shoes to homeless people around the United States. She first conceived of the idea while watching news reports in the aftermath of the September 11, 2001, terrorist attacks on the World Trade Center.

"I was watching a CNN report about Afghan soldiers. As I watched, I noticed that most of them had no shoes." At that moment, Kristina said, the concept for SOLE PURPOSE was born.

As a runner (from a family of runners) who once ran five miles every day, it's not surprising that Kristina would see value in a pair of sneakers that others might not. But there were challenges. So Kristina and her mom began to brainstorm.

"We wanted to deliver shoes to the Afghans but didn't know how to get them there," Kristina said. "So I began to research locally and found out that a homeless person wears out a pair of shoes every six to eight weeks and there are more than 350,000 homeless in the state of California. The need for shoes is endless!"

Kristina decided to place her initial focus on helping the homeless and needy in Southern California, then consider branching out to cities across America. She formally launched SOLE PURPOSE in February of 2002. There were frustrations at first—but door-to-door denials and corporate roadblocks strengthened Kristina's resolve. She soon discovered that neighbors hosting

garage sales were quite eager to give away old shoes
by the dozen. A local running store helped out, and
Kristina set up a table at local races. She printed up
flyers and set up a Web site. Soon some marketing ideas
kicked in, and before Kristina knew it, she was being
featured in *Runner's World* magazine, on the *Sharon Osbourne
Show*, and the *John Walsh Show*. In her first two years,
Kristina collected over 7500 pairs of shoes.

She collected shoes from running clubs and track teams,
from police officers and firefighters, from marathon
runners and people who simply enjoy a weekend stroll.
She has delivered them to shelters in Los Angeles and
throughout other parts of Southern California.

"There's an enormous number of kids and adults in
need of simple things like shoes," said Diana Vogelbaum,
director of a shelter in Camarillo, California. "They're
on their feet all the time. When they sleep out in the
open, they're nervous about taking off their shoes
because someone might steal them."

When Kristina picked up shoes from any location, she
first inspected what she had. Those that were too tattered
to be of any use were thrown away. Others accumulated
in large piles in the family garage, added to by the pairs
collected by Kristina's "shoe crews," or teams of friends
who worked with her. When the piles became too big,
it was time for the shoes to be delivered to the shelters.

The work Kristina started is spreading across America.
New Shoe Crews and other SOLE PURPOSE groups have
popped up in thirteen states and in Canada. Kristina

receives new inquiries every month. Collectively, SOLE PURPOSE groups donated thousands and thousands of pairs of shoes. And it seems the work will continue until, as Kristina hopes, every homeless individual in America has a pair of shoes on his or her feet.

"Someone asked me if there's still a need for more shoes," said Jan Radnoti, Kristina's mother. "I thought to myself: They must be living in some kind of bubble."

Now a college graduate, Kristina remains excited that people from all over want to help. She said she keeps an open invitation for anyone to join in and start their own Shoe Crew to help make a difference.

Her encouragement: "I'll help you get started!"

LAURA

Hillenbrand

In 2003, the feature film *Seabiscuit* was one of the most acclaimed movies of the year. The story of the underdog horse that captivated the nation in 1938 captivated the nation once again through its retelling on the big screen.

The film's success was a tribute to the fine work of author Laura Hillenbrand, who wrote the 2001 best-selling book titled *Seabiscuit: An American Legend*, the work from which the movie was adapted. Hillenbrand gained notice for the fine writer she was, but also drew attention to the parallel story line that existed in the story she penned and the one she lived. Perhaps it was her ability to see so much of her own experience, character, and spirit in the famed horse that enabled her to achieve such great success in telling the story. For like the great champion she wrote of, Hillenbrand herself is an overcomer.

While she wrote *Seabiscuit*, Hillenbrand suffered through a terrifying ten-year cycle of health problems that made normal life challenging and writing improbable. Her illness didn't go away while she wrote, but at times she was able to forget her circumstances and lose herself in the characters from which she drew inspiration. Her ordeal began in 1987, when she was just 19. She became ill on a road trip back to college. She ran a high fever, couldn't eat, and had trouble walking short distances.

"First, my legs would weaken and I'd lose the strength to stand," Hillenbrand wrote in a 2003 article in *The New Yorker* describing her struggle. "Then I wouldn't be able to sit up. My arms would go next, and I'd be unable to lift them. I couldn't roll over. Soon I would lose the strength to speak. Only my eyes were capable

of movement. At the bottom of each breath, I would
wonder if I'd be able to draw the next one."

Over the next few years, various doctors informed her
that the mysterious illness was purely psychological,
putting Hillenbrand through an agonizing period of
blaming herself for her symptoms. Finally, she found
a doctor who took her seriously and diagnosed her with
CFS, or Chronic Fatigue Syndrome.

Experts describe the illness as a complex disorder
characterized by debilitating fatigue that is not improved
by bed rest and that may be worsened by physical or
mental activity. It affects blood pressure, weakens the
immune system, and can make mental concentration all
but impossible. Victims often feel useless and defeated.
Many give up hope of regaining a normal life. Because of
her illness, Hillenbrand dropped out of school and was
unable to handle the rigors of full-time work. She was in
despair.

Seabiscuit came along just in time. Hillenbrand always
loved horses and wrote for equine magazines when
she had enough strength. One day, she came upon
information on Seabiscuit's jockey, Red Pollard. Further
research led her to fall in love with the story of three men
beset by hardship who reassembled their lives around the
little horse.

"I could definitely identify with them," Hillenbrand
said. "Red lost his family. Charles (Howard, Seabiscuit's
owner) lost his son. And Tom (Smith, the horse's

trainer) lost his world. Me, I lost just about everything to this illness. I lost my future."

Hillenbrand attacked the story with all the passion she could muster. Writing was a way to momentarily escape her circumstances and the pain of her existence.

"I got very emotionally involved in telling this story," she remembered. "Living in my own subjects' bodies, I forgot about mine. My emotions would mirror whatever part of the story I was researching on a particular day."

Hillenbrand found ways to write despite her illness. "When I was too tired to sit at my desk, I set the laptop on my bed," she wrote. "When I was too dizzy to read, I lay down and wrote with my eyes closed."

Seabiscuit earned numerous honors and won critical acclaim as one of the top books of 2001. More important, it gave Hillenbrand a platform to spread awareness of CFS and provided a pathway for the author to get past the years of lying in bed wondering if she would live to see tomorrow. She found a door of opportunity for a new life.

"When I was writing, I became a storyteller, not an invalid. My entire life wasn't oriented around my body. My life had a purpose to it . . . . I felt like I was living for the people I was writing about . . . . The whole world is new to me."

MARY JOE

Fernandez

Mary Joe Fernandez was once considered a tennis prodigy. She was also known as a woman of her word.

One teaching pro called Fernandez "the most mentally tough person in the history of tennis." Another predicted she would become "the best ever." The praise came in volumes—all before Fernandez even received her driver's license.

Fernandez earned this admiration by winning four straight Orange Bowl junior titles and, as a 14-year-old, becoming the youngest player—male or female—ever to win a match at the U.S. Open. As a young teenager, she was hotly pursued by agents, tournament organizers, coaches, and corporate giants. Everyone wanted a piece of Mary Joe.

But Fernandez had entered the pro tennis world insisting she would never let the game take precedence over her education. Few believed her. Wait until the major titles and big paydays come, they thought, then we'll see the importance school really holds. The press waited for Fernandez to fold. They assumed it was only a matter of time before she turned her back on her promise. That's when she did something completely different.

With the allure of a professional career at her command, Fernandez stunned the tennis world by announcing her intention to stay in school and earn her high school diploma. She would play only in events that did not interfere with her education.

In an age of tennis academies and high-pressure training, where secondary education is truly secondary to the shaping of a pro career, Mary Joe's decision ran counter to the lure of prize money and endorsements.

Demonstrating surprising maturity and foresight, she held to her commitment, saying "There's always time to play tennis afterward. An education balances out your life and gives you something to fall back on."

It was clearly a challenge to juggle school and a professional tennis career, but Fernandez managed to excel at both. She maintained an A average throughout junior high and high school, while still ranking in the Women's Tennis Association (WTA) top ten.

After graduating from high school in 1989, she prepared for her first full season on the pro circuit. In January of 1990, her preparation was rewarded when she reached her first Grand Slam final at the Australian Open. By the end of her first full year as a pro, she was ranked No. 4 in the world, with two tour wins and a semifinal slot in the U.S. Open.

With health problems plaguing her throughout her brief career, Fernandez decided to retire from competitive tennis in 1999.

Her accomplishments were significant: she won over $5 million in career earnings and earned top-ten season rankings six times. She appeared in two Australian Open finals and one French Open final and was regarded as one of the top five women's tennis players during the '90s.

More important, Mary Joe Fernandez gained a
reputation as a person of integrity who kept her promise
to herself, never allowing tennis to become more
important than her education.

CONSUELO CASTILLO

Kickbusch

Retired United States Army Lieutenant Colonel Consuelo Castillo Kickbusch is a woman with a gift to lead and a passion for young people. She rose from very humble beginnings to become a woman of significant influence. However, before she could impact others, she had to learn to respect herself.

Born and raised in a tiny barrio in Laredo, Texas, Kickbusch overcame the severe challenges of poverty, discrimination, and illiteracy to become a model of success. Breaking barriers and setting new standards in the military, Kickbusch rose to the position of senior officer and became the highest-ranking Hispanic woman in the Combat Support Field of the United States Army.

Known as a charismatic, passionate, and entertaining speaker, today Kickbusch takes her powerful life message of respect and leadership to colleges, corporations, and government institutions in the United States and abroad.

"I was born on the third to the last street of America," she said. "Not everybody gets up every morning and looks at another country. I found myself seeing the Mexican-American and the Mexican and American cultures at once."

During her distinguished military career, Kickbusch held a variety of demanding and critical leadership positions, ranging from Executive Officer for Information Systems Command to Technical Advisor to the Joint Command and Control Warfare Center to Company Commander of an all-male platoon.

She earned numerous decorations, including the Legion of Merit, the National Defense Service Medal,

Meritorious Service Medal (four times), the Army
Achievement Medal (twice), and the National Image's
Uniformed Services Award for significant contributions
in the areas of civil and human rights, race relations,
equal opportunity, human resources, and public service.

In 1996, Kickbusch was selected from 26,000 candidates
to assume a post that would put her on track for
General Officer rank. She declined the honor, retired
as a twenty-year veteran, and founded Educational
Achievement Services to realize her personal dream of
helping people of all ages succeed.

Because of her dedication to saving American youth
living in the same barrios she did as a child, Kickbusch
has worked with over one million children, parents, and
educators in the roughest neighborhoods in America.

Such a distinguished career looked unlikely during
Kickbusch's upbringing. One of ten children growing
up in a poor family, she learned that self-respect has
little to do with wealth or poverty. She also learned that
success, security, and happiness can be found in any
circumstances as long as self-respect exists.

"Poverty should never grant you a license to act, think, or
behave poorly," Kickbusch said. "It's far more important
to be rich in soul, heart, and mind."

"I grew up with what I call a set of core values. They were
never negotiable," she added. "They were etched in stone
as far as what my parents would consider the standards—
courtesy, respect, integrity."

Much of Kickbusch's foundation of values came from her mother, who worked as a maid. Her model instilled in Kickbusch a clear sense of self-respect. She recalls her mother telling her, "Every morning my room is identified as being the cleanest, the best, well-done. That's my pride . . . . I don't expect you to clean toilets. I expect you to, whatever you go after, to do it to the best of your ability."

Her immigrant father also had a profound impact on her self-esteem and her perspective. "He said, 'This is not my country, but it is yours. If you can give nothing to it, take nothing from it. We don't come here for handouts. And if you must sacrifice something for it, even your life, then so be it.'"

Those words of wisdom stuck. From a core of self-respect, Kickbusch has not only realized personal success, she has also passed the lessons on to millions of others.

"We can all make our dreams come true, to not give up hope, but rather to take charge of your lives," she said. "Make a real difference in your families and communities and follow a disciplined road map to success."

ILA

Borders

All her life, Ila Borders was told she would never be able to do it. She was told her dream was ridiculous. That she should give up this wild idea and go back to doing things girls are supposed to do. She endured verbal abuse of fans, snickers from teammates, catcalls from opponents, and mockery from the media. Still, Ila never lost sight of her dream. And in the realization of that dream, she never lost her self-respect.

In 1997, Borders became the first female to play in men's professional baseball when she pitched for the St. Paul Saints of the Northern League. Borders' historic moment came on May 31, 1997, when, as a relief pitcher, she entered a game against Sioux Falls. She recorded her first pro victory later that year and helped lead the Duluth-Superior Dukes to the league championship with a 1.97 earned run average.

Borders continued to play professionally through the 2000 season, when she announced her retirement. Her professional career was marked by the media circus that at times surrounded her and ran rampant with tabloid stories about ulterior motives behind Borders' effort to crack the pro ranks. Unfazed, Borders steadfastly told reporters she played the game for one reason only.

"I'll look back and say I did something nobody ever did," said Borders. "I'm proud of that. I wasn't out to prove women's rights or anything. I love baseball. Ask a guy if he's doing it to prove men's rights. He'll say he's doing it because he loves the game."

A high school baseball star in Southern California, Borders was Whittier Christian High School's Most

Valuable Player and became the first woman ever to earn
a scholarship to play men's collegiate baseball when she
was signed to a letter of intent by Vanguard University
(formerly Southern California College).

While her physical attributes were not the equal of her
peers in the Northern League, Borders succeeded because
of her intelligence, composure, and strength of will.

"She threw a fastball probably 72 to 73 mph, and her
curveball maybe 58 mph. Most everybody has to throw
an 87- to 88-mph fastball and a curveball at least 77
to 78 mph," said Borders' manager, Mike Littlewood
of the Zion (Utah) Pioneerzz, during her final pro
season. "She knew how to pitch."

Because of that and because of what she had to endure,
Littlewood said, Borders should be judged by different
standards than other baseball players. "Ila was one of
the most courageous people I've ever met or seen play
the game," he said.

In her three years in the game, Borders dealt
with prurient inquiries from the press—no, she did
not shower with the guys—and outright harassment
from fans.

"I've been spit on, had beer thrown on me, and been
sworn at, and was hit 11 times out of 11 at bats while in
college," Borders said upon her retirement. "But the
memories I have are the ovations when I would run in
from the bullpen."

Through it all, Borders never lost her sense of identity or perspective on what she had accomplished.

"I happen to think it's pretty fantastic that I'm the only female to ever play baseball with the guys," she said.

Olivia Bennett is living her dream. She is a world-renowned artist whose paintings sell for as much as $20,000 apiece. She has appeared on *Oprah*, published a book, and sold her paintings to many prominent people, including former President George W. Bush.

She has already achieved a level of success that most artists can only hope for, having been compared to masters such as Georgia O'Keeffe and Claude Monet—all before the age of 20. As a teenager, she opened her own studio and art gallery and was named by *Teen People* as one of the "twenty teens who will change the world."

On top of it all, she is a leukemia survivor.

Olivia started her art career with a set of Crayolas when she was just a toddler. "When I was very little—two or three—in coloring books I was doing way beyond what kids my age were doing," said Olivia.

Her mom was quick to encourage Olivia's talent, buying more books and supplies.

"When I was five or six I really started getting into watercolors and getting serious about painting," Olivia said. "That was all I wanted to do. I wasn't playing or watching TV. I was just painting all the time . . . . I still remember my very first painting. It was a watercolor of a vase of purple flowers. And my mom did what most other moms would do—she put it up on the refrigerator."

But just when she had discovered her love for art, doctors gave Olivia's parents the startling diagnosis. Olivia was just five years old.

"I went in for a kindergarten checkup and they found something in my blood," remembered Olivia. "They said 'This looks a little off' and they diagnosed me with leukemia." One doctor gave little hope for the future.

Two years of intensive treatment followed. During Olivia's chemotherapy, one side effect of an experimental medication caused temporary nerve damage.

"The medicine I took . . . made my hands curl up into claws," she said. "It was horrible. Painting became a release for me. I didn't have to think about going in to get a spinal tap the next morning."

She first painted a basket of flowers her mom had bought at the grocery store, and she immediately took to the imagery. Painting flowers became a form of physical therapy for Olivia.

"It's something about the colors. I painted one, and I was just in love," she said.

Her hands eventually healed and, at age seven, Olivia's doctor said she was finally cancer-free. With improved health, Olivia spent even more time on her artwork, and painting began to turn into more than just a hobby.

"Before I knew it, it had developed into my passion," she said.

Soon Olivia was creating magnificent art that astonished those around her. Friends and family speak of a glow that came over her face and how her spirits lifted dramatically when she painted. With the cancer gone, the artistic gift that was uncovered during a time of deep adversity was now in full bloom. Today flowers remain Olivia's specialty, and many of her works hang in homes all over the world.

"I think no matter what, I would have become an artist," Olivia said. "Being sick just kind of helped me discover my passion sooner rather than later. And it helped me focus in a way that just a typical life without cancer might not have. And it made me really appreciate that every moment is a unique and rare opportunity, and I should just take advantage of it. That's what I try to do with some of my paintings."

Olivia spends seven to twenty hours completing each individual painting. Every one serves as an expression of her love for life itself.

"Paintings are a symbol that we care and feel for others," she said. "Each painting I finish for someone is like a constant reminder from me to them that no matter what happens in their life, there's always hope, and they should just always believe."

DR. SALLY

Ride

Riding in a spacecraft traveling 17,500 miles per hour, floating suspended in weightlessness, and exploring the boundaries of the universe . . . Who wouldn't want to become an astronaut?

That is precisely what Dr. Sally Ride thought when she first learned that NASA was looking for people to be a part of the space program. In 1978, Sally was working on her doctorate degree in astrophysics at Stanford University when she read a NASA advertisement seeking astronaut candidates, and she was on her way to making history.

She was among the more than eight thousand men and women who applied to the space program that year. Of the 35 individuals accepted, only six were women. One was Sally Ride. Five years later, she made history by becoming the first American female to go into space.

As a young girl growing up in Los Angeles, Sally was drawn to the physical universe and often dreamed of going to the moon. "I was always interested in science and math," she said.

But she temporarily found an outlet for other talents. She was a standout youth tennis player, at one time ranked nationally on the junior circuit. She put tennis aside at Stanford, though, where she earned four degrees: a Bachelor of Arts in English, a Bachelor of Science in Physics, a Masters in Physics, and a Ph.D. in Physics.

Sally was accepted into the astronaut corps in 1978 and completed her training as a mission specialist in 1979. On June 18, 1983, she made her historic trip when she orbited Earth aboard the space shuttle Challenger.

As the first American woman in space, Sally broke
a major gender barrier.

"NASA just realized, and the government realized, that
women could be astronauts, not just men," she said,
noting that in the early days of the space program, NASA
used military-trained test pilots. "There were literally
zero female test pilots at the time," she recalled. "As time
went on, NASA realized there was nothing special about
men being astronauts."

She made a second flight aboard Challenger in 1984
and was training for a third mission when Challenger
exploded in January 1986 with its crew aboard. She was
appointed to the Presidential commission investigating
the accident.

When the investigation came to a close, she went to work
at NASA headquarters in Washington, D.C., as assistant
to the administrator for long-range planning. There she
created NASA's Office of Exploration and wrote a report
on the future of the space program entitled "Leadership
and America's Future in Space."

In 1987, Sally left the astronaut corps to join the faculty
of Stanford. Concerned about the lack of female scientists
and engineers, Sally was eager to find a solution to the
problem. Her goal was to identify and teach other women
who could follow in her footsteps.

In 1989, Sally joined the faculty of the University
of California at San Diego to teach physics and serve
as the Director of the California Space Institute. She was

also appointed as a member of the President's Committee of Advisors on Science and Technology and served on the commission that investigated the 2002 Columbia space shuttle tragedy.

As a pioneer, Sally Ride is a model for other young women who share her childhood dreams of going into space. While she continues to inspire others, Sally still marvels at what she accomplished: travel to space and inspire a generation of young women to follow her lead.

"When I was a little girl I always dreamed about flying in space," Sally said. "Amazingly enough, and I still don't believe it to this day, that dream came true."

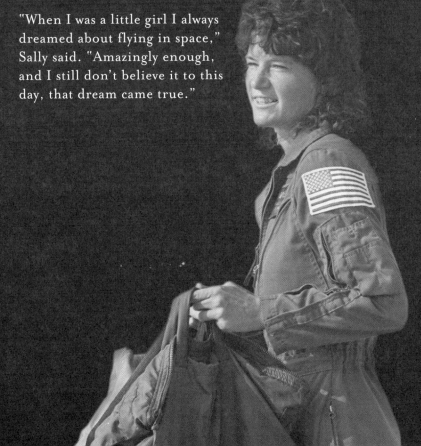

U.S. WOMEN'S

Softball Team

In their 2004 run to the Olympics with a record of 53-0 against the best collegiate and amateur softball teams in the nation, the U.S. women's softball team was nothing short of amazing. At the 2004 Summer Olympic Games, they defended their gold medal in overwhelming fashion, winning all nine of their games with a combined score of 51-1.

Because of their dominance on the field, they were called the "Real Dream Team" on the cover of *Sports Illustrated* during its pre-Olympic coverage. Looking at the stats, it's not hard to see why. Once they hit Athens, they broke 17 Olympic records (nine of which they already held or shared) and tied another on the way to their third straight gold medal. The pitching staff registered a microscopic 0.12 ERA and threw 55 straight scoreless innings. They pitched eight consecutive shutouts with five straight one-hitters. Their nine straight wins (a record in one Olympics) extended their international winning streak to 79 straight, dating back to July 13, 2003.

But their story of teamwork goes beyond the scoreboard. They supported their head coach, Mike Candrea, during the most difficult time in his life—and this may have been the team's biggest accomplishment of all.

Less than two weeks before the team was scheduled to leave for Athens, Candrea's wife, Sue, suddenly became ill. She was rushed to the hospital, where doctors determined she'd had a brain aneurysm. She died two days later. Sue had quit her job to travel with the team and was like a mom to the players. Her death was devastating to the entire team.

"Coach Candrea is a second father to all of us and Sue was like our mom on the road," said star pitcher Jennie Finch. "It was incredibly hard for all of us, but we leaned on each other for strength as each of us searched for answers to this unbelievable tragedy. We knew Sue would want us to continue and travel to Athens to take home the gold."

Ten days after Sue Candrea's death, the team boarded a plane for Athens without their head coach, who arrived a week later after dealing with his wife's death and funeral arrangements. While the players mourned the loss of their special friend, rather than just go through the motions during the Olympics, Team USA bonded even closer together through the adversity. They vowed to help fulfill Coach Candrea's goal for the team.

"I don't want to just win," he told them on many occasions. "I want to dominate."

Candrea drew strength from his team and the memory of his wife's goal for him to coach in the Olympics. He stressed to each of the players to treasure each moment. Memories of his wife kept him focused as they pursued a shared dream.

His final encouragement to his team was stirring: "I don't want you to play for me or Sue during these Olympics, because this is about representing your country and playing for the United States of America."

The team responded. Beginning with a 7-0 victory over Italy, Team USA ripped through the tournament, not allowing a run until the gold medal game against Australia in their 5-1 victory.

"To me courage doesn't mean you're brave," Mike Candrea said following the Olympics. "Courage is something that allows you to get through tough times. I told this team from day one that they could be special athletes. They proved to me they're not only special athletes but special people."

YULIANA

Perez

It is remarkable that today there is a smile on the face of Yuliana Perez. During an adolescence marked by grief, loss, and discouragement, with seemingly no hope for the future, smiles were mostly nonexistent.

Yuliana was just three when she watched as her mother was killed in a drive-by shooting. Because her father was serving time in prison for robbery, Yuliana was moved to foster care for two years before being forced to leave sunny San Diego and sent to Havana, Cuba—the birthplace of her parents—to live with her paternal grandmother.

"Living in Cuba was hard," said Yuliana. "My mother left Cuba to be in the United States to give me a better life. When she died, it wasn't fair."

Although she found comfort with family, Yuliana was confronted with a difficult situation. Yuliana had blossomed into quite an athlete, and Cuban sports authorities saw the lanky teen's extraordinary abilities and trained her, first as a sprinter and then a triple jumper. By 1999, Yuliana was good enough to be included on the Cuban team that would compete in the World Championships. But when Cuban officials demanded she give up her U.S. citizenship in order to secure a spot on the team that would represent Cuba at the 2000 Summer Olympics, Yuliana refused. Officials promptly kicked her off the national team, dropped her from their elite program, and removed her from her sports school.

Suddenly she was a woman without a country, and it appeared that her dream of becoming the best female triple jumper in the world was over.

"I was young and really good and asked if they were going to give me money each month to pay my expenses," said Yuliana. "They told me no and I said that's my answer for you—I was not going to change my citizenship."

Because she was born in Tucson, Arizona, Yuliana held American citizenship. She longed to get back to the U.S. but did not know how to make that happen. Sports became secondary to a fruitful life.

"I was under a lot of pressure and I was really hurt. I wasn't in the sport for entertainment. I was in it because . . . I needed it to live. They were joking with my feelings and that wasn't fair. They didn't want me and I didn't want to stay anymore."

It took five months to get help, but finally the Swiss embassy in Cuba arranged for Yuliana to receive a U.S. passport. Though she no longer knew anyone in America, Yuliana traveled on her own back to Tucson in early 2000, arriving with only a backpack and a referral to a foster home. With the help of a foster care worker and an inquisitive Tucson bus driver, Yuliana found the route that would eventually take her to college and the Olympics.

One day, while adjusting to her new life and language, Yuliana took the wrong bus and wound up talking to the bus driver about her experiences. When she told him she had been a track performer, he directed her to Pima Community College, where his friend Mario Peña was a coach.

"She pretty much felt there wouldn't be any more chances," said Pima coach John Radspinner. "She was so happy she got lost on the bus one day, because it turned everything around."

Within a year, Yuliana was the national junior college champion in the long jump and triple jump. In 2002 and 2003, she became the national champion in the triple jump and was ranked No. 1 in the U.S. and No. 3 in the world. In 2004, she competed for the United States at the Summer Olympics in Athens.

"She's an amazing athlete as well as an amazing person," said Radspinner. "She is so dedicated, and when she realized that she now had another chance, it motivated her beyond the level that she was already motivated to. She has such a high internal drive. When she sees an opportunity, she takes it and goes with it as much as possible."

Yuliana overcame long odds to become a champion. In the process, she became a model of desire, determination and dedication who refused to let obstacles deter her.

"I'm not going to stop until I get my dream," Yuliana told the *New York Times*. "I'm going to train and work hard until I get there. My dream is going to the Olympics— one, two, three times."

JEAN
Driscoll

When Jean Driscoll was born with spina bifida, doctors painted a bleak picture. They told her parents that as a result of the congenital birth defect—characterized by the incomplete closing of the spinal column—Jean would most likely never walk, have to be enrolled in special education classes, and be dependent on them for the rest of her life.

But Jean Driscoll proved the doctors wrong.

More than thirty years after that fateful pronouncement, Jean Driscoll is now one of the world's most decorated athletes. When she won the wheelchair division of the Boston Marathon in 2000, it was her eighth title in the prestigious race. With her commitment to excellence and her indomitable spirit, Driscoll has become the most celebrated female wheelchair athlete in America. She has even been "jogging" with President Clinton.

Because her condition occurred at the lower end of her spinal cord, Driscoll was able to walk with leg braces from the age of 2 until she was 14. She staggered awkwardly from side to side, dragging her feet and struggling to keep her balance. She insisted on being included in neighborhood games and races and excelled at crawling through obstacle courses. She loved playing H-O-R-S-E and perfected the art of shooting a one-handed basket with her right hand while holding on to a fence for stability with her left.

In fourth grade—against the advice of her parents—Driscoll taught herself to ride a bike. One Saturday, she rode up and down the sidewalk in front of a friend's house for eight hours. At the end of the day, she rode home to show her parents.

"I can ride a bike!" Driscoll screamed as she rode by.

"You're going to break your neck!" her mother screamed back.

"I don't need my training wheels anymore!" she proudly responded.

Still, there were numerous reminders that she was different from other children. She remembers the days her sister and three brothers would take turns pulling her to grade school in a red wagon. She remembers how her mother made her wear rubber boots over her shoes when she went to the playground, to keep the blacktop from destroying her leather shoes. She remembers riding her new ten-speed bike, falling on her left hip and dislocating it. After five operations to strengthen the joint and a year in a body cast living in either a hospital or her family's living room, the hip dislocated again when the cast was removed.

"I was told I'd end up with a sit-down job," Driscoll said. "My only goal was to sit behind a desk, filing and typing. My sister could be the first female President, but I was supposed to become a secretary."

Doctors said that because of her lack of lower body musculature, Jean would have to use a wheelchair and crutches to get around. When she returned to school at 15, her peers began to make fun of her because of the wheelchair. She was devastated by the entire experience, fell into deep depression, and even contemplated suicide.

"It was a blow you couldn't believe," she recalled. "I was very angry for several years. I couldn't make myself comfortable with the chair. I would ask God, 'Why don't You pick on somebody else?'"

In the end, though, it was the wheelchair that removed barriers and enabled her to start living. "I thought, 'Now my life is over,'" Driscoll said. "But the thing I thought would limit me has enabled me more than I ever imagined. I've done what most people only dream about."

She became the best wheelchair racer in the world. She set world records or world best times in sprints and endurance events. Her strength and stamina would make an ironman competitor jealous. She medaled at the '92 and '96 Olympics, as well as the '96 Paralympics. But the road to success as an athlete was formed through great despair.

"My disability was always an excuse. It was the reason I didn't get the boyfriends I wanted and the reason I didn't get babysitting jobs as early as my sisters."

While in school, Driscoll tried to find herself in academics, but even that went awry. She flunked out of the University of Wisconsin-Milwaukee after three semesters.

During her academic hiatus, Driscoll met the person who would be the catalyst for extraordinary changes in her life. During a year spent as a live-in nanny for a young family, Driscoll met then University of Illinois coach Brad Hedrick. Hedrick had spoken at a wheelchair sports clinic and watched Driscoll and others play a game of wheelchair soccer. Something caught his eye.

"I saw lots of enthusiasm and talent that was unchanneled at the time," Hedrick said.

"He saw my speed and thought that could transfer over to the basketball court," Driscoll recalled.

Soon Hedrick began recruiting Driscoll to come play wheelchair basketball at Illinois, the nation's top program for wheelchair athletics. With no hesitation, she grabbed the opportunity.

From 1987 to 1991, she lettered four times and won three MVP awards for the Illini women's wheelchair basketball team, helping them to the national championship in '90 and '91. She was named amateur athlete of the year by the Women's Sports Foundation in 1991 and has been honored with Jean Driscoll Days in Champaign, Illinois, where she now lives, as well as in Milwaukee and in the state of Wisconsin. On top of all that, she graduated with distinction in speech communication in 1991 and received her master's in rehabilitation administration in 1993.

Driscoll's success in racing was built upon the foundation of her faith and the confidence she gained from her impressive career at Illinois. She began to train for racing and quickly became a major force.

A Milwaukee businessman donated a racing wheelchair for Driscoll's first national race, the Phoenix Sun-Times 10K. With little training, Jean took third place and gained a new respect for wheelchairs. She began winning races of varying distances all over the world. She came home from her first international event in England with nine gold medals.

It took Driscoll's coach, Marty Morse, two years, however, to convince Jean to enter a marathon before she debuted at the

1989 Chicago race. Morse's gentle persuasion helped Jean stay on track. She finished eight seconds under two hours in Chicago, qualifying her for the Boston Marathon in 1990.

"But I don't want to do any more marathons," she moaned to Morse following the Chicago race.

"You don't qualify for the Boston Marathon and not go," he told her.

She went. She also won the race in Boston in world record time. It was the first of seven consecutive victories in the sport's most prestigious race and the beginning of an amazing career.

"If you're willing to take risks, to dream big, and work hard, you'll meet goals you never thought you could," said Driscoll. "So many people have a fear of failure. It paralyzes them."

What makes Driscoll so good? Her commitment to training is legendary. Around Champaign, her nickname is the "Jean Machine." She logs as many as 130 miles a week.

"I plan my life around my training schedule," said Driscoll. "I love being in shape. I love being fit and strong."

None of her workouts compare, however, to Jean's hill repeats. She usually asks someone to hang on to the back of her chair until she's so weighed down she practically spins her wheels—usually three to five people total onboard.

At 5-foot, 110 pounds, she has the best strength-to-weight ratio of any woman in the sport. She has huge deltoids, bulging biceps, and taut triceps, and she bench-presses 200 pounds and can transfer that power each time she pushes the rims on the wheels of her chair. Her power enables as many as 130 revolutions per minute while maintaining an average speed of 16.5 miles per hour. Because she is so light, she attacks hills with relative ease. Because she is so fearless, she thinks nothing of descending at close to 50 miles per hour. This has served her particularly well in Boston, where the marathon is well-suited for her strengths.

"Racing at Boston is a spiritual experience for me, more so every year," said Driscoll. "It's a big deal to win there. It's the race I want to win. I've placed a bigger priority on it than even the Olympics. I look forward to it every year. I feel stronger each year I race at Boston."

Aside from her physical prowess, what makes Driscoll a champion is her heart and her mental toughness. She developed a unique ability to concentrate as a child, spending long periods of time attempting to keep her balance and stand still.

"For most of my life, too many people placed limitations on me," Driscoll said. "Well, I'm making a living at a sit-down job, but it happens to be wheelchair racing."

Driscoll is sometimes recognized when out in public, but with the recognition has come responsibility. Driscoll is clear about her desire to be a role model to all people. She signs autographs with her personal motto, "Dream Big and Work Hard," a to-the-point message of her life—the same message inscribed in large letters across her bright yellow racing chair. Jean Driscoll has discovered that the words "you can't" have become a challenge to find a way.

"God has given me an incredible platform and I'm really enjoying using it," she said. "For young people and adults, the biggest limitations are the ones you place on yourself. You have to experience failure before you can appreciate success.

"I am not a disabled person. That's not how people define me. I'm not a courageous person. I'm an elite athlete who's training for the same reasons as [any other world-class athlete]. I want to be the best in the world in my sport. I want to make a difference."

GAIL

Devers

In the early nineties, Gail Devers was the world's top female sprinter. Watching her, one would never guess that just a few years before, she could barely walk.

In May 1988, Devers set a U.S. record in the 100-meter hurdles at 12.61 seconds and qualified for the U.S. Olympic team in the event. But in Seoul, she ran inexplicably poorly, failing to make the finals. Afterward, she sank into a mysterious illness.

For almost two years, Devers suffered from vision loss, wild weight fluctuations, fits of shaking, and nearly perpetual menstrual bleeding. For two entire years, Devers was practically bedridden—and no one could explain why. Finally, she was diagnosed as having Graves' disease, a thyroid disorder. But the radiation that doctors used to destroy a cyst and the bad part of her thyroid gland ended up destroying the whole gland. Her feet began to swell and ooze; her skin cracked and bled. The pain became so unbearable that her parents had to carry her to the bathroom.

The world's finest sprinter had been reduced to an invalid. The feet that carried her to some of the fastest times in history were now on the verge of requiring amputation. But thankfully, before those world-class feet were lost, doctors realized that the radiation treatment may have been to blame. The same doctors told her that two more of days of walking would have meant amputation. Devers's therapy was changed, and in a month she was able to walk again. It was the beginning of the greatest comeback in track history.

Once back on her feet, Devers worked tirelessly at regaining her Olympic form. At the 1991 world championships in Tokyo, she placed second in the 100-meter hurdles. Then her golden moment came at the 1992 Summer Olympics in Barcelona. The world saw that Gail Devers had neither died nor lost her mind. Her hair had grown back, her weight was steady, and she was competing in the Olympics—running on feet that once couldn't walk. Devers won the 100-meter dash by inches in Barcelona and with it the title of the world's fastest woman.

During Devers's darkest time, her coach, Bob Kersee, once called her at 2 a.m. He'd had a dream, he said. And in the dream, he saw Devers with knees left bloody when she climbed up rocks to get out of water. To him, the dream meant Devers could come back, but only at a price.

She paid that price eagerly, and though she now says that while she wouldn't wish Graves' disease on anyone, she is "very thankful for having gone through it."

Dealing with the illness, she said, taught her she can deal with anything.

Devers went on to repeat as gold medalist in the 100 meters at the '96 games in Atlanta, and again lost out on gold in the 100-meter hurdles. She missed out on a chance to three-peat in 2000, but by then her story had been etched into the sports world's annals and the nation's consciousness.

"You can't have an ounce of doubt, because that doubt will eat you up," Devers said. "Now I have total faith in

myself . . . going through what I've gone through, there's
no obstacle that I can't overcome."

In politics, if you want anything
said, ask a man. If you want
anything done, ask a woman.

Margaret Thatcher

DR. KATRINA

Poe

One of just 900 residents, Katrina Poe grew up in the small town of Kilmichael, Mississippi. When Katrina, the daughter of a garment factory worker, was in the fifth grade, she decided that she would go to medical school, become a doctor, and return to her hometown to practice medicine.

"I think it's important for me to care for people, because that's what I was born to do," Dr. Poe said. "I am supposed to provide care for people in need. I feel that it is a service to my community and I want to do a good job."

Her desire to give back has long been front and center for Katrina. Many times throughout her teenage years, she told her family and friends that she would come back to help out the people of her hometown.

"Most physicians who come from small towns usually go to larger cities," she explained. "So everybody was surprised when I came home, but that had always been my dream even before going to medical school."

After medical school, Dr. Poe returned to practice medicine at the local hospital, the Kilmichael Clinic. She was not only the primary physician in Kilmichael, she was also the town's first African-American female doctor.

"It was challenging in the beginning," she said. "There were patients who initially refused to see me because of my race and some even because of my age and even my [gender]. But with time people have adjusted and I don't see that problem anymore."

Even with the early challenges, it didn't take Katrina long to learn that she was where she was meant to be.

"I love my job; I love what I do," she said.

That passion gives her strength to persevere and focus when the hours get long.

"If you ask any of the staff members, they'll tell you I'm really committed to my patients," said Katrina. "Being the only physician, I am on call twenty-four hours a day, seven days a week and it is hard."

Dr. Poe finds that she must often work 80-hour weeks in order to accommodate the needs of her patients. In addition to being a doctor, she is also a wife and the mother of two children—and this kind of schedule can be challenging to her young family. Still, she remains driven by her passion to help the people of her community.

"It's an internal clock that wakes me every morning, because I know there's a job to be done," she said. "But I don't see it as a job—it's truly fulfilling for myself as well. And I think that's a wonderful professional achievement, just being a family doctor here in this town."

Because of the love she has for her profession and her patients, Dr. Poe earned the respect of those in her community. She took the time to get to know her patients personally and build relationships with them. Many residents refuse to see any other medical professional.

"I feel that I have a very good relationship with my patients," Katrina said. "I think one thing that enhances that [relationship] is that I am from this small town. So we immediately have something in common."

The small-town environment necessitates a different kind of approach than might be found among doctors from large urban hospitals. This is part of what Dr. Poe enjoys most about her job.

"Being a physician in a small town, there are occasions when you have to make house calls and that takes a lot of time from your already busy schedule, but that's a wonderful experience," she said. "You learn a lot about their family, which aids in your ability to take care of them."

From clinics to house calls, Dr. Poe finds her job extremely rewarding. In 2005, her commitment to Kilmichael earned her the Country Doctor of the Year award—a national honor created to recognize the spirit, skill, and dedication of America's rural medical practitioners.

"It was a great honor to be awarded the Country Doctor of the Year award," she recalled. "Everyone here was just so ecstatic, but it was more humbling to learn that I was the youngest recipient of the award."

As Dr. Poe continues to work tirelessly in her community, she hopes that others will be inspired by her example; that they will dream big, work hard, and develop a passion for their jobs. She also hopes her example will encourage others across America to commit to give back to the people of their own communities.

DR. SALLY
Knox

Breast cancer is a devastating disease. But Dr. Sally Knox is doing everything she can to lessen that devastation.

Dr. Knox, a surgical oncologist at Baylor University Medical Center in Dallas, is one of the leading breast cancer physicians in the world. She specializes in surgical procedures for gravely ill female cancer patients. Dr. Knox has found success treating her patients and helping them defeat the disease; she has also found ways to help cancer patients who don't have medical insurance.

Dr. Knox is literally a lifesaver who says her success comes from a treatment method that not only deals with the physical aspects of the illness but the emotional side as well.

"Usually the first thing a woman thinks when she is diagnosed with breast cancer is, 'Oh my goodness, I'm going to die,'" Dr. Knox said.

According to Dr. Knox, when a patient learns of her diagnosis, the reaction is typically very emotional and ranges from anger to fear to depression. Dr. Knox has found it vital to offer her patients peace, comfort, and hope in discussing their treatment options and outlook for the future.

"Because it isn't just a physical illness—it affects our emotions, it affects our spirit as well—it's a whole person not just a physical body there," she said.

Therefore, Dr. Knox has taken a whole-person approach to dealing with her patients. She handles each situation uniquely. She recognizes the fine line she walks with a given patient.

"I try to emphasize to [each patient] the positive things about that—just the fact that women will be treated successfully. And we can't promise that as physicians, but what I do encourage my patients to do is to take each day one at a time."

By helping her patients through the emotional trauma of the diagnosis, Dr. Knox is able to help them realize they can get through it. She has seen more of her patients grow stronger through the process than those who shrink in fear.

"What I have discovered, and what my patients have taught me time and time again, is that they grow deeper and they grow richer in their understanding," she said.

Dr. Knox is not only committed to helping those who come into her office but also has extended assistance to those who are less fortunate.

She founded The Bridge, a nonprofit organization helping uninsured women who have breast cancer. Through this outreach, she is providing financial assistance for women who would otherwise receive no help and perhaps no treatment.

"We started The Bridge back in 1992, because I wanted to make sure that as a medical profession, we took care of women in that situation," Dr. Knox related. "They have a lump in their breast or something abnormal and they have no resources. They are either uninsured or underinsured and they don't have the capability of getting the treatment. I really felt like as a society we have a responsibility to expand our resources and help those women."

Through the organization, Dr. Knox said hundreds of women have been helped and lives have been changed. "It's been very gratifying," she said. "Those are very grateful patients."

The prospect of fighting cancer on a daily basis is challenging for Dr. Knox. While not every woman makes a complete return to health, she remains encouraged by the vast majority who survive and even thrive.

"People have asked me, 'How can you remain in this profession and see cancer day after day and tell this person that they have breast cancer?'" she said. "What makes it really rewarding, what makes it really worthwhile, is that you see these people move through the process and get better and come back and their lives are back intact again. They're back traveling or working or whatever it is that they enjoy doing."

Helping women handle and get through their times of crisis is more than a vocation for Dr. Knox. She feels it is a calling and says that it is what she is most passionate about.

"It takes a lot of courage to get through breast cancer— both on the part of the patient and her family—and to be a part of that and to be an encourager in that has profoundly impacted me."

about the author

Steve Riach is a principal and founder of SER Media, a Dallas-based media company. He is an award-winning producer, writer, and director of numerous television, film, documentary, and video projects, and is one of the nation's foremost creators of virtuous and positive-themed sports content. Steve's programs have been seen on ESPN, FOX Sports, NBC, and a variety of broadcast and cable television outlets. He is also the principal behind the creative vision for the Heart of a Champion® brand. His start in sports media came as an on-air personality, hosting national television and radio programming.

A prolific writer, Steve has authored *Passion for the Game, Above the Rim, The Drive to Win, Inspire a Dream, It's How You Play the Game, Life Lessons from Auto Racing, Life Lessons from Golf, Life Lessons from Baseball, Heart of a Champion: Profiles in Character,* and *Amazing But True Sports Stories, Amazing Athletes Amazing Moments,* and *Par for the Course.*

Steve is also the cofounder of the Heart of a Champion Foundation, a nonprofit organization devoted to producing materials designed to instill character and ethics in youth. Steve is creator and author of the foundation's innovative Heart of a Champion® Character Development Program, a leading tool for the character education of students in schools, after-school outlets, and juvenile justice programs across America.

A former college baseball player and a cancer survivor, Steve is also a sought-after speaker to education groups, youth agencies, schools, corporations, sports organizations, and faith-based organizations.

A native of Southern California, Steve and his family now make their home in Colleyville, Texas.

**If you have enjoyed this book,
Hallmark would
love to hear from you.**

Hallmark Book Feedback
P.O. Box 419034
Mail Drop 215
Kansas City, MO 64141

Or e-mail us at
booknotes@hallmark.com